ALEXIS LEVI:
BOARDROOM TO THE LOCKER ROOM

**The First African American Woman To Own
A Men's Professional Basketball Team**

**Written by Alexis Levi
and compiled by Karyn Schofield Darnell**

authorHOUSE®

AuthorHouse™
1663 Liberty Drive
Bloomington, IN 47403
www.authorhouse.com
Phone: 1-800-839-8640

Published by AuthorHouse 2/5/2013

ISBN: 978-1-4772-7528-3 (sc)
ISBN: 978-1-4772-7527-6 (e)

Library of Congress Control Number: 2012917992

DEDICATION

Thank God that this journey is on the rise again. First and foremost I want to thank Abraham and Gladys Levi, the best parents a girl could ever have!

Next my wonderful sons Deavereaux and Tyler, may your success be fulfilled. Thank you for your support and love through the tough times. May you always know you are the most important to me in this world.

To Greg, thank you for standing by me during the toughest time of my life, the loss of my mother. To my Aunt Eloise, I appreciate all that you have done for me, my mom and the boys.

To my uncles, May God Bless you for your support. And to Auntie JoAnn you're the best . To the Las Vegas Stars, I am grateful for your belief in me and the fact you always gave it 100%.

The International Basketball League, I appreciated the opportunity to live out my dream. Thank you for your support during the ups and downs. I will never forget you all as I continue on this journey.

Thank you to all my Linked In Family our reach is over 50 million people! My Facebook Friends, Pepsi ,Ebony Magazine, Essence Magazine, N'Digo Magazine, Luxury Magazine and Las Vegas Community and all my national and international supporters.

ACKNOWLEDGEMENTS

God is always first!

Deavereaux and Tyler: The best sons in the world!!

Greg Marshall, Randy Larson, Karyn Darnell, Karen Waters, Deb Hayter, Dan Savage, Hollis Hale, Darren and Rhonda Dorsey, Ms. Dee Dee and Family, Karen, Eloise McDaniels Mt Zion Spiritual Temple Ms Elie Perzinger, Pastor Duley at Kaleo Christian, Pastor House at Mountaintop, Gail Anderson, Lydia High, Bobby Gasper, Bobby Bowden, Camille Bradshaw, Carmen Villalobos, Cindy Bekale, My Sports for Life Family, National High School Basketball Association, Sports Management Worldwide Family,

INTRODUCTION

It is time to realize everyone has a God given purpose to influence those around us whether we are young or mature. Life comprises many twists and turns, we often experience trial and error, disappointments, frustrations and set backs which clog our lives leaving us feeling defeated and hopeless. However, it's time to stand up and rekindle those impossible dreams in your relationships, career, and spiritual walk.

To be a happy successful individual I have learned to live by a few well-known quotes:

- Make the Best Out of Today Because Tomorrow Is Not Promised
- No Matter What You Go Through God Has Got Your Back.
- Look Forward, Don't Look Back
- Live by Faith Not By Sight
- Wake Up Every Morning And Say Thank You
- Be Grateful For What You Have
- Today Is The Only Day, We Can Count On
- We Are Not In Control Of Our Destiny

In this book, you will discover-the journey of a woman destined to be the first African American Woman to Own a Men's Basketball Team

- The Ups and Downs of Running a Business And A Basketball Team

- How to Rise To The Top Through Adversity
- What It's Like To Be A Woman in The Sports Industry
- How to Live Your Dreams
- The National & International Rise of the Las Vegas Stars
- Overcoming the Obstacles

I want the readers of this book to walk through my life, often times people think that someone that makes it to a degree of success did so without trials and tribulations.

As you will see in this book, I endured lots of pain and suffering during my life. The message that I would like for readers to understand is that you must not give up.

If I had of given up, I would have never received the blessing. After enduring the Early Loss of a Parent, Physical Abuse, Loved One on Drugs, Single Parenthood, Loved one with Cancer, Near Death Experience and Infidelity, I knew that it was my faith and hope in my future that was able to get me through.

ENDORSEMENTS

Alexis is more than a sports pioneer, she's a visionary and a born leader. She's not afraid to think outside the box and put those ideas into practice. She's knowledgeable, personable, professional, and competent.

Arif Khatib
Founder/President
Multi-Ethnic Sports Hall of Fame

Alexis is one of the most driven, professional, and giving people I have ever met. From our first conversation, it was evident that she was going to succeed in any endeavor Alexis started. It's been a great pleasure to collaborate together, help support each other, and work together on numerous projects.

Scott Manthorne
Co Founder
All Sports United

Alexis, I admire what you are doing in the business and basketball world.

Rick Barry
NBA Hall of Fame

TABLE OF CONTENTS

CHAPTER 1
Overcoming the Odds

The Las Vegas Stars led by Alexis Levi the 'First African American Women' to own, act as CEO and General Manager of a Men's Professional Basketball Team. The team was made by the power below.

Dajuan Tate: A story within himself was paralyzed after a fall while playing basketball. He was back on the court jumping through the roof, an amazing act to watch.

Matt Winan: From the World Renowned Gospel family, a top basketball player who later went overseas; and became a member of the practice team for the Miami Heat.

Eddie Shelby: The kind of player every coach would want, plays hard, dunks the ball, athletic, a playmaker.

Waki Williams: Tough player who always fought to the end

Herve Gibson: Tough player who always fought to the end.

Hollis Hale: A three point shooter with an undeniable shot, a team leader.

Willie Hall: The captain and point guard of the team was the glue that held it all together on the floor.

Deavereaux Vinzant: 6ft 8 only played a few exhibition games because of his college eligibility and sprained ankle.

Trevor Lawrence: 7 ft Center always giving the guards a hard time.

Maurice White: Quiet off the court but an aggressive player that came off the bench to back up Willie Hall.

Sean Higgins: NBA Veteran came on board to bring true NBA Basketball Talent. Though he only played a few games the fans received a treat watching him shoot NBA Range 3 pointers that showed nothing but net.

Willie Hall: Team captain the general on the floor keeping the team together and generating the plays, 6 ft 1" always needling the big guys, "the prankster."

The Beast: Though only with us for a moment, his size allowed us to dominate in the paint. This was the start of something powerful an undeniable force.

And of course the team's biggest fan: Tyler Larson my youngest son always eager to miss a day at school to be on the road with the Las Vegas Stars.

Crowd in a buzz...2007

As I sat and looked around the gym at the teams, the stands, the crowd in a buzz, the referees preparing to begin the game, I realized this was it. What we had been waiting for, to begin our journey as a first year professional men's basketball team. The Las Vegas Stars had made it!

The referee's whistle blew the time clock sounded signaling to the players it was time to go to the bench. Lights gleamed from the score board, the sports castors readied to announce the opponents. The national anthem bellowed as each player stood motionless in respect and complete attention to salute the American Flag. The players prepared for what would be the first of many appearances at the playoffs for the Las Vegas Stars, I was astounded by the moment. Moments later the coach called the first five players to take the floor. I questioned, "How did I get to this point in life?" My mind flashed back to my childhood.

Father's Love...

I remembered times when my parent's and I were at home together. Every Sunday morning we'd go to church as a family. After church Dad would throw on some Jazz or Blues records. My parents would hum the tunes and recollect their younger years. Mom would say, "Honey, do you remember when we danced the night away?" He'd close his eyes recollecting their bebop times as a smile surfaced. They talked about the music artists who performed at the popular venues of their time like the great Duke Ellington and Chubby Checker. Of course, they boasted the music of their day, "Now that was real music."

Mom would be cooking in the kitchen. Suddenly, she'd burst from the kitchen with a sway in her hips, fingers snapping and singing her favorite tune. She drew dad in with inviting eyes. He'd jump to his feet, understanding the invitation, and quickly turned up the volume on the 45 record player. They'd dance, whirling with speed and rhythm, dodging furniture and the dog with ease and precision. My parents loved to dance. The flaming duo persisted, swinging to and fro. Then finally they jolted to a riveting stop for a final bow. She'd slowly trot back to the kitchen with a gentle sway in her hips, humming beneath her breath. I was a captive audience and clapped with anxious anticipation. It was my turn, he grabbed my hand and away we'd go. He was the greatest dad in the whole world and I was his little girl.

A fighter...

I was an only child, born on March 24 in the sixties to Abraham and Gladys Levi.

They tried to have a child for twelve years and just when my parents decided to adopt, my mom started feeling real funny. "Oh yes," she was pregnant. Mom told stories about how Dad got sick just like she did during her pregnancy. She'd say he was having "sympathy pains."

When she felt nauseated, so did he. When she gained weight, his belly bulged with a rounding girth.

The doctor called me a miracle baby because Mom had fibroid tumors. I was actually positioned behind them and squeezed as I tried to grow. My grandmother said, "Your father was told he had to make a choice which one the doctors would save in case of an emergency, mother or baby?" My father being an honorable man responded, "I can't make that decision. Let's put life in God's hands."

I was born weighing 4lbs 12 oz, a FIGHTER. I stayed in the hospital for a few extra days due to my premature size. My Grandma sat and rocked me saying, "Bootsy, bootsy, bootsy." Therefore my nickname was born, "Bootsy." Dad said, "She's so tiny I can fit her in the palm of my hand." My grandma told stories of how dad cherished me but was afraid to pick me up with his big clubby hands. He'd say, "Hold her up so I can see her." Then my mom would scoop me up from the crib and show me off. He'd inspect my tiny hands and feet and gaze at my features. Then he'd smile nodding in satisfaction whispering, "My Bootsy." Fears of somehow crushing me in his strong grip haunted him, so until I gained weight he was cautious. My dad was a big teddy bear of a man, strong in character and integrity. As the years passed there were times mom swore my dad and I were one. She'd get mad and he'd smooth things over.

He was the oldest of ten children. His family was Jewish and he was raised going to temple and celebrating the Jewish holidays. When he met my mother he accepted Christianity while maintaining his Jewish heritage. He was a responsible man and forfeited his education to help raise the rest of the family. Later, he joined the military where he learned to be a top mechanic on military planes. I inherited his entrepreneurial spirit as he owned his own car repair shop. He began working on friends cars and after a while there was such a demand he decided to open his own auto shop: Levi Automotive. Then he decided to apply for a head security position at the Oakland Coliseum. A job he took so he could watch the Raiders, A's and the Warriors at no additional charge to his wallet. My Dad was a sports fanatic and we shared the passion together, especially basketball. As a little girl, I spent a lot of time watching the A's and the Warriors.

Like a sister to me...

As a child I first attended Fairview pre-school, where I met my best and oldest friend Karyn Schofield. She was one of nine kids her house was like being at an amusement park. There were constant clouds of commotion and boisterous activity in the house and out in the yard. It wasn't unusual to see kids climbing through the windows, walking on fence tops and retrieving balls from the roof. There was always a game of 'one foot over the gutter' or 'red light-green light' clogging the streets. Bikes, skate boards and even homemade scooters whistled down the side walks accompanied with screams of warning to those unaware, "Move it or lose it."

Karyn was like a sister to me. Since I didn't have brothers and sisters it was such a change in atmosphere to go from a quiet, controlled environment to the Schofield's bustling, unpredictable, explosive house teeming with adventure. There never was a shortage of kids wrestling, throwing an elbow or a kick while intersecting several games simultaneously. The neighborhood mimicked a school playground with packs of kids roaming according to age. The back kitchen door slammed in rhythmic action as sweaty kids scampered in and out. Her mother, Mama Lo took it all in stride. Once the house was loaded with kids and her father yelled with impatience, "Tell all the neighbor kids to go home." Mama Lo looked around and said, "Robert, these are all our kids."

One day after school I went to the Schofield's house and played with all the brothers, sisters and neighborhood kids. After a few hours my Mom pulled up in her big yellow Cadillac. Her facial expression read fear as droves of kids covered the neighborhood riding bikes and playing various games. She was frantically searching for me among all the children. Karyn and I ran in the house because I wasn't ready to go home. Mom popped her head in the kitchen as if to say, "Where is my child? Is she still alive?" Karyn pointed to me, "She's right here." I popped under one of the kitchen chairs and protested, "I'm not going home." "Alexis, get out of there, right now," Mom complained.

One day a neighbor man came to visit my Dad. He was very militant, Pro Black, borderline prejudice. He'd try to encourage my Dad to only fraternize with Blacks. My Mom and Dad had lots of friends from all backgrounds. I remember one day Karyn was at the house playing after school and this same neighbor came over. I warned her, "Go and hide because that man doesn't like little white girls." Karyn looked at the man in fear and scampered past them. You know Karyn was a little white girl and I knew he would have something to say if he saw her on our property. She hid on the side of the house and soon my dad followed behind asking, "What are you doing back here?" Karyn replied, "I'm hiding because that man doesn't like little white girls." My dad laughed out loud and said, "You're our guest, there'll be no hiding on our property."

Daddy never let his skin color or others determine who he would associate with or what he would become. He worked hard, took care of his family, and influenced the community through service that was his witness and mission. My parents were very social and enjoyed many friends. My father was the head of the Knights of Columbus and my mother the Catholic Daughters at All Saints Church.

Devastating change...

On December 18, 1971, my life changed forever. I fell asleep before Dad came home but Mom always waited up for him. After coming through the door he smiled and leaned over to kiss her soft cheek while she warmed his dinner. He retreated to the family room where he often sat to eat his dinner worn and tired after a long day. He ate, she watched. They enjoyed TV, laughed and talked about the day. Afterwards they went into their bedroom and retired. "I need to use the bathroom," Dad groaned. He got out of bed nursing a limp with a leg cramp. He sat on the toilet, "My leg is throbbing." A few minutes later a large hard knot developed on his neck. Not knowing what it was he asked, "Baby, please rub my neck?" He tried to get up and make his way back to bed but fell short stumbling to the floor. My mom panicked and pulled with all her might but her 5ft 5in, 110 pound frame couldn't budge his tall, husky body. She called Mr. Bradley next door as well as 911 to get an ambulance. He slipped into a coma and was transported via ambulance to Eden Hospital in Castro Valley, California. He lay unconscious in Intensive Care intubated. Early the next morning my mother woke me up to share the tragedy. I was in shock, "How could he take me to school in the morning and not be there when I woke up the next day?" Devastating change was knocking at our door.

Slipping away with Angels...

Mama let me visit Dad in the hospital before he went to the other side. I remember holding her hand as we walked into a cold hospital room, with floors shined, and a curtain pulled around his bed. I peeked around the curtain fearing what I might find. There he was lying on his back between white starched sheets, arms carefully positioned at his sides, with closed eyelids puffy from fluid retention. He looked like he was sleeping, if it wasn't for all those tubes, pumps and monitors. Daddy had a tube in his mouth connected to a machine. Every time the machine took a breath, then Dad took one. It was the strangest thing I'd ever seen. Mom slowly released my hand as I stepped closer to his bed. She knew I needed to figure this out for myself. "Daddy," I whispered reaching for his big clubby hand that held my whole body when I was born. His hand was still warm but where was all the movement? Daddy was such a hard worker, his hands were always moving but now there was no response. My heart sank as my eyes searched for some glimmer of hope. "Daddy, it's me Lexi, wake up it's time to go home now." The nurse whispered to my Mom, "There was no brain wave response from the EEG (Electroencephalogram). So she shouldn't expect any response." Of course, Mom never told me that grim news. I repeated, "Daddy, wake up it's time to go home." I slipped my hand into his and pulled it to my wet cheek. For the first time in three days he showed a sign of understanding by squeezing my hand. The nurses couldn't believe it and marveled at any response. Later that day, Dad slipped away with the angels. My mom was alone and never saw the love of her life's waking eyes again.

Why God why? ...

"How could I help?" The pressures of life experienced to young can be crushing. "Are you okay Mom?" I tried to sooth her and then hid a flood of tears. It seemed I grew up overnight. "What did it mean to grow up and be an adult? I didn't know but I was going to do my best and be there for Mom. I was only 10 years old and just getting the hang of being a kid. Now I had to assume another role. When all the family, friends and associates left, I knew it would only be me and my mom. I went from being a child to a strong force in my mom's life overnight. I felt an inner responsibility to take care of her.

The day of the funeral was surreal. It felt like I was floating outside my body watching a parade of sorrow march by. Hundreds looked down at me with crumpled faces, tears streaming and noses red from blowing. This was the day I would say goodbye to my Dad forever. "How could this be?" I really didn't have a chance to get to know him. "How could God do this to me? Did I do something wrong?" my mind searched for an explanation. I remember seeing kids with a mom and dad and thought, "I must have done something really bad for God to take my Dad away." Later, I was told by my Auntie, "Your Dad was such a wonderful man that God wanted him in heaven. He needs good people in heaven too." Even though I didn't understand completely, it made me feel a little better. I remember crying for days on end, I'd sneak into the bathroom or the closet so my mom wouldn't see me. I wanted her to think I was strong, so she'd be strong.

All this for Dad...

The funeral was held at All Saints Church in Hayward, California. There were hundreds of people, standing room only. As my mom and I came through the church doors, I noticed men and women lost in a flood of emotion. The Knights of Columbus were in their full attire as they lined up along the aisle. Each knight was wearing a large hat, with black, red and silver capes, swords were drawn while "Amazing Grace," was playing. Military guns were sounding off out side. The American Flag was draped over the casket. I remember thinking, "All this for Dad." It was like he was the President of the United States.

The pallbearers wore white gloves and clutched the silver handles on the casket tightly. They moved slowly, methodically carrying the marble gray casket to the front of the church for the service. I remember Dad looking just like he was sleeping, with rosary beads in his hands. At one point in the service Mom and I approached the open casket. It was the last time I would reach for him in the natural. However, throughout the years I've reached and called for him many times through the spirit. I touched his hands and face but this time he was ice cold. "Don't worry, I'll take care of Mom," I whispered. His absence left a deep vacuum in my soul.

It wasn't until years later I fully came to realize the love, peace and contentment only my Heavenly Father could bring into my life. God my Father had given me the best earthly father a daughter could ever dream of, even though it was only for a short season. Losing my earthly father at such a young age was catastrophic but God used it to eventually build sensitivity to His Spirit and relationship with Him. My soul is content knowing I will meet my father again because my Heavenly Father holds him securely. This has brought great contentment and hope. It was amazing, all night everyone kept saying, "Your Father was a great man."

Dad's voice echoed...

After the funeral, life resumed. Over the years I reflected back to a pointed conversation I had with my dad a few months before his death. We'd often take long drives on Sundays into less fortunate areas. Then we'd drive back over the railroad tracks and head for the elaborate neighborhoods in the hills. He'd tell me about his personal adversities. "I only had a sixth grade education and helped raise my brothers but through it all your mother and I have been blessed. We have properties, cars, and all the toys. I want you to always dream big and go for whatever you want in life." Dad paused then continued, "Now, listen little girl, don't let anyone tell you your goals can't be achieved. You're an African American and can accomplish anything with God's help."

His words echoed in my mind and heart throughout the years, especially when my inner critic screamed negativities. Dad's voice resonated, like waves saturating dry ground, encouraging and motivating me to push ahead despite the odds or circumstances. He'd often say, "Don't let anyone rob your purpose or destiny." His heart and voice are still resounding today propelling me on to be a person of impact and destiny.

A hunger to achieve...

For a first year team the thought of playing in the International Basketball League Playoffs was unbelievably outrageous, most thought. Others believed it to be scandalous that we could make it. Some wanted to label us as lucky. I'm sure most thought somehow we were undeserving because most of my players weren't noted for being former NBA stars they were ex-college players and overseas professional players.

However, in my opinion that's what made this whole season astounding and miraculous. The Stars were basically comprised of men with a hunger to achieve their goals and a vision to succeed. Few held grand titles with vast accomplishments behind their names.

The thought appealed to me during the try outs months before; this team was handpicked by God. I couldn't have imagined what a powerhouse of a team was born and gelled together through trail and error our first year. The players believed in me and it was reciprocated.

We battled literally through the press and locker talk from the other teams the whole season. My athletes weathered the pop, cynical comments from other managers and players. "Playing for a woman?" one player sneered. "She doesn't know what the hell she's doing," others from opposing teams scoffed. "I wonder what player she's sleeping with?" a manager joked. Of course, reports of all the negativity flowed in through multiple sources but I refused to ingest the poison. We began formulating what would be a team that had former NBA players, the son of a Basketball Icon as the Coach, and past Continental Basketball and International Team Players. The press began to report, "Who is the woman in Las Vegas? She obviously knows what she's doing and has taken a different strategy." The Interviews came in and the commercials began to run.

Yet, cheap shots and accusations continued to flow like waves of toxic poison. But we were on 'Top of the World,' what an exciting time but jealousy and envy lurked in the shadows. Several investors had come forward to assist us in the venture of owning the professional team. We began to hire additional front office staff to secure the support of the team. Practices were intense in preparation for what would be the biggest and toughest journey of my life.

The Public Relations Team began to work closely with the staff to develop what would be the biggest promotional event for the launch of the Las Vegas Stars. Within ten days, Deb Hayter event planner extraordinaire had pulled together a celebrity cast of attendees from Los Angeles and Las Vegas. The event was held at the exclusive Stirling Club and in attendance were 400 people, the newspapers, TV Networks and more.

The morning of the event 'the guys' were so excited to actually be introduced to the market they would play for. Many of the team members were unknowns from across the US. But after the event they would be the talk of the town.

It was all new to me being the Owner, General Manager and Chief Executive Officer of a professional men's basketball team. My past experience running businesses and working in corporate America prepared me for the difficult, grueling task. Investors for the team had flown in to participate in this great event. This occurred the day before the team would play their first game. Well the event went off without a hitch and the Las Vegas Stars were definitely on the move.

When the season began we were at the gym bright and early preparing for the day. Excitement was in the air and we were ready to play our first opponent the "Phoenix Flames." The players all met at the Center at 10am, each were to check in with Player Development Staff to receive their uniforms and daily stipend. Once the last player was checked in the tour bus pulled into the driveway. The Stars had to travel instyle; we boarded the luxury coach full of excitement and glee. Laughter and joy echoed through-out the bus as we took the four hour drive to Phoenix, Arizona. The closer we got to Phoenix the louder the chants got "Las Vegas Stars, Las Vegas Stars!" We pulled into the lot, the forum where the Phoenix Suns NBA team used to play, parked the coach and filed out heading to the locker room.

As the Las Vegas Stars walked on the floor I could hear dad cheering from the grandstands in heaven, "Don't let anyone define who you are, or what you can achieve. Be proud you are an African American and a Woman." I looked up with a smile, "Thank you daddy." God still does miracles today!

CHAPTER 2
HOOP Dreams!

Attending Catholic School was a rewarding experience. In grade school I played most sports from basketball, volleyball, softball, to cheerleading. I also competed in ice skating. I was a feminine girl with a competitive spirit. It was during these growing years I learned to play basketball. I was the tallest girl on most of the teams and liked to win. My coaches were awesome, fair to the players and positive whether we won or lost. They were like my best friends. They would push me to do my best never attempting to break down my self- esteem or humiliate in front of others. I applied these same principles when dealing with the Stars and the players responded gallantly. Realizing the competitiveness and the bureaucracy of the sports industry, I attempted to always remember my players are humans and I treated them as such. I believe this is why they always gave 100% on the court.

Reswponsibility to inspire...

I attended Moreau Catholic High School it was actually ranked second in the nation. There were a lot of wealthy families, some kids came to school in limousines and wore the finest clothes on free dress day. I had a lot of friends from all ethnicities and backgrounds. Though I came from an upper middle class family I was always pretty down to earth.

I began to work in my sophomore year at Sears Regional Business

Office, it was a great job. I was making over ten dollars an hour and saved for my first car. By the time my senior year rolled around I saved enough money to purchase a new car. I remember going down to the Pontiac dealership and thinking I would only have enough for a small car. When we walked through the door, I spotted a Silver Formula Firebird with t-tops. I paused and immediately motioned to my mom, pointing to the Sunbirds.

My mom asked me to step outside while she completed the paperwork. The next thing I remember she handed me the keys to a brand new Formula Firebird. I was so excited to take it to school the next day. "I purchased it myself," I told my friends. By first period I was the talk of the school. Then other kids began to work to get their dream car. Even back then I felt it was my social responsibility to inspire and help motivate those around me. I found it to be rewarding not only for myself but for those who were encouraged and went on to accomplish the unreachable.

He weaves His purposes...

During my senior year of high school I attended the Fairmont Licensed Vocational Nursing Program. Karyn and I met up again after being separated due to busy schedules and going to different schools. We attended All Saints Catholic School together until 7th grade. She ended up going to public school from junior high through high school.

I remained in private Catholic school and graduated from Moreau High School in 1979. I gladly picked her up many a dark winter morning in my new car. We had to arrive early at the hospitals for report on the patients. We were on the road by 6:00 am, now that's early for high school kids.

I pulled up slowly to Karyn's blue house with the salmon pink trim. The house was dark and quiet for a change with only a single light on in the kitchen. 'Mama Lo' was up preparing breakfast for her large family and just escorted her husband out the door for another day of work. I honked a few times; Karyn walked out in a crisp white nursing dress with freshly painted white shoes. She hopped into my car and off we went. As we drove down the road she cleared her throat. I looked over at her slightly while still keeping my eye on the road. "Alexis, I want to thank you for picking me up. If it wasn't for you I don't know how I'd get to the hospital in the morning. I want you to know I appreciate what you're doing for me." I nodded, "No problem, you'd do the same for me if you had a car."

She smiled back and eventually we both completed the program. I never realized the impact we would have on each other in the years to come. God puts specific people in our lives for many reasons. Some come for short seasons and for specific purposes in order to teach us lessons in life, to refine or define us. Unfortunately, at times we plant and cultivate toxic relationships never intended in the first place. Then we wonder why our lives become so chaotic, disruptive an unproductive. You have to look for those impact friendships and relationships in your life to fully develop into the person of destiny you're meant to be.

I was always told by my mom nursing was one of those careers you could always count on for job security. My mother was a smart woman and married a great man, my father! She was strong willed and taught me to never give up the fight; to always make smart decisions and establish a firm foundation for my family.

So at 19 years old, I finished school and became a License Vocational Nurse. I began to work and the pay was pretty good. I decided to further my nursing career and began taking classes in the summer at Chabot College. I transferred over to California State University of Hayward and began working towards my RN license. My days of college were great, I had been under the structure of Catholic School for over 13 years. I could finally exercise my independence. I was very fortunate my dad set up a college fund. One day I was thinking about dad and realized he was buried between the high school and college I attended. Moreau High School was on the side of the cemetery and Cal State East Bay Hayward sat on a high hill above the cemetery. It was almost like he had a premonition he would not be there to share those years with me. My Dad must have known that sports would play a big part in my life because he definitely took me to as many pro-baseball, pro-basketball and pro-football games as he could while still on the earth.

CHAPTER 3
Loss of Love

Until this point I rarely dated and never experienced a serious boyfriend. One Saturday night I decided to go out with a few friends. One of my girlfriends, Eunice who was not yet twenty one asked me to take her boyfriend Tony along with the group to a club named "Silks." This was the largest, hottest club in Northern California. People from all over the world came to Cali to go to "Silks." It had five dance floors, three DJ's, and packed hundreds of people in the doors for all night parties.

I picked Tony up and Eunice told us to have fun and politely whispered in my ear, "Keep an eye on him." It was a warm California night, we had the t-tops off, the music was blaring, "The men all paused as we walked into the room," this was our theme song. Tony hopped in the crowded car saying, "You girls are crazy." Laughter erupted and we sped off.

We parked and walked to the front of Silks there was a line around the building. I was able to get us in VIP style because I was popular at the club. I was a dancer similar to some of the movies of today like, "You got served." I walked up to the security guard he said "How many with you tonight?" I said, "Eight." They patted us down and then let us through the door. Tony laughed saying, "You got in like that?"

We pulled a few tables and stools together and made enough room for all of us. We danced a few songs and then we sat back down. I looked up and the finest guy in the world walked through the door.

He was about 6'3, fair-skinned with dark curly hair and a moustache. I remember telling Tony, "Now he's fine!" Tony laughed and said, "He just looked over at you." I said with an anxious smile, "He did." Tony smiled, "He keeps looking at you. Why don't you go over there and ask him to dance?" "Are you kidding? I can't do that! He probably thinks I'm with you. Scoot over, you're sitting to close. You're messing up my game," I complained. Tony and I laughed and before I knew it the handsome stranger disappeared into the crowd. "Damn, he's fine," I couldn't shake the thought and definitely wanted to talk to him. In moments he reappeared to the same spot and this time our eyes met. I smiled, he smiled. We danced towards each other and looked away in embarrassment.

Tony reappeared jokingly, "Aw, you guys are so cute! Girl, go over there and ask him to dance." All I remember is looking away from my friends for a moment and Tony decided to be funny and pushed me off the bar stool. I stumbled like a real klutz. He kept pushing, "Go ask him to dance?" I was paralyzed with embarrassment but felt compelled to move in the stranger's direction. "Do you want to dance?" my voice quivered at my own boldness. He said "Sure."

My heart sped up. "Okay he was fine and nice, there had to be something wrong," I thought. He probably couldn't dance that would spoil everything. We began to dance, "Okay, he had rhythm, oh thank God, he could dance." He actually was pretty good. We danced ten songs straight. I think it was right then I fell in love with John Deavereaux Vinzant. He was 6'2" tall, medium built, fair skinned with hazel eyes and curly hair. He was mixed with Italian and Black and we all know that's a good combination.

Happy yet, Dad not there...

From that point forward, we spent lots of time together and dated exclusively. He was a great person. We were the envy of all of our friends. He was respectful, loyal and very loving. When I was with him, it appeared I was the only one in the room. We began to talk of spending the rest of our lives together, we were in love. I was still in college, so we decided to get engaged and marry after graduation. We set our wedding date for Valentines, 1984. Our colors were red and white.

The morning of the wedding I awoke euphoric, only one thought dampened my glory, "My dad wouldn't be there to walk me down the aisle," tears welled. I asked my dad's best and longtime friend to do the honors. I had to believe Dad was there in spirit. As I dressed for the wedding Mom came to the room, "You look beautiful, your dad would be so proud of his Baby."

Early in our marriage John and I received a message a little miracle was coming the latter part of the year. Yes, I was pregnant and scared about starting my own family. This was the first time I'd given my heart to a man since my dad and didn't want to experience another loss. Our son Deavereaux Vinzant was born on November 16, 1984, 7 lbs, 12 0z. We called him "Dev" for short. He was everything to us, our pride and joy.

When John looked at Deavereaux, there was a love like I had never seen. This was the year everything was going to be perfect. We had a beautiful condominium, nice cars, money, a loving relationship and a beautiful child. We opened up our joint checking accounts and of course we had our own separate accounts too. Momma always told me, "Make sure you keep a side account for a rainy day." Luckily, I did as time passed John changed.

Out of control...

At first, I thought it was the pressure of all the responsibilities. John worked long hours and lots of overtime to make sure we had enough. One day I stopped by the bank to draw some money out and our account balance was lower than it should have been. I asked the bank teller to print an activity summary and low and behold there had been several withdrawals from the ATM machine. I looked at the dates and times of the withdrawals. They were all made when John was supposed to be at work. I called a girlfriend to vent and questioned, "No, he isn't spending our hard earned money on another woman?" "I'm sure there's an explanation," she replied.

When he came home from work I blasted with accusations while sitting on the couch tapping my fingertips. He came in smiling, "Hey baby how was your day?" I said, "My day was fine, until I went to the bank and found out all the damn money's gone!" He began to explain as most men do when they're caught. "Baby, I needed the money, it's mine not just yours," he angrily retorted. "I realize that... but we agreed to let each other know when we needed to take extra out of the account," I bellowed in frustration. "How are we going to pay the bills?" I flashed with anger. We fumed for a few minutes John still refused to disclose why he needed the money. "Are you taking other women out?" I probed. "No Baby, you know you're the only one for me," he replied in his usual loving manner.

What he said was partially true. I found out later, one incident after the other that John had a substance abuse problem. He admitted to it one day after another incident of unauthorized bank withdrawals. "What's going on again? What excuse is it this time?" I blasted throwing the bank receipt in his face. Slowly, he looked away dropping his lunch pail and jacket on the kitchen table. "I'm addicted to cocaine," he admitted. Instantly, I began to cry, "How was I going to control this?" my mind questioned.

Several days earlier John complained he was experiencing pain in his scrotal area. He noticed some swelling and asked me to look at it. To my disbelief his scrotum was the size of a tangerine which is an indication of a severe problem. I immediately called the doctor and made an appointment for evaluation. After seeing the doctor he was instructed to sit in a bathtub to reduce the swelling. A few days later I came home from work at around 8 am, I was a night shift nurse. John was lying on the couch appearing glazed and critically ill. "I think something's really wrong," his voice was weak and concerned. He proceeded to show me his scrotum it was the size of a large orange.

Around this time I called Alta Bates Rehab Center and talked to them about John's drug problem. He realized he needed professional help to clean up and kick the habit. I made an appointment and we packed his bags and went to the hospital. We consulted with the nurses and the doctors, John agreed to enter the program. When we started the admitting examination, I asked the doctor to take a look at John's enlarged scrotal area. The doctor looked concerned, "Let's do some testing," he stated.

A few days passed and we anxiously awaited the results. John remained in the Rehab Center for the next few nights. I'll never forget the feeling I had in the pit of my stomach the day the doctor called and delivered the sobering news. I was busy running around the house when the phone rang, "Would I answer it?" Looking at the phone I realized fear was controlling me, I had to answer it. "Yes, Alexis speaking," my voice cracked under the stress of the previous weeks. "Hello, this is your husband's doctor from the rehab center. He gave me permission to call and discuss his condition with you." I braced and collapsed on the couch quickly. "Your husband has testicular cancer," He apologetically.

Our life together began to unravel quickly without any means to prevent the onslaught of approaching pain. As the doctor spoke, my muscles flinched, forgetting to breath, my chest tightened. There it was again like instant replay, a man in my life that I loved was suddenly being taken away. My mind raced in a thousand directions, "What would become of me and my son? Would I loose John forever?"

I dropped the phone and cried uncontrollably. What an awful time, I learned my husband was addicted to drugs and had testicular cancer within a few short weeks. Plus I had a toddler to chase after, and worked full time. I asked my mom to watch Deavereaux and rushed to the hospital. My girlfriend Deborah drove, I was too hysterical.

Upon arriving John was sitting in the TV room. The doctor bustled in the room and asked us to join him in his office. As the doctor elaborated on the bleak lab findings, we began to cry together. He explained, "The type of cancer you have is more prevalent in white males." Even more alarming was the statistics, there was only a 50% chance of survival.

We decided to move forward with the surgery and chemotherapy. It was a trying time, John was so sick from the chemotherapy. During this process, they found another touch of the cancer in his lung area which totally terrified us. We prayed night and day and through it all John had a positive attitude. He never believed the 'doctor's report' about death. He focused on living and the future. As God would have it, he came through with flying colors. The surgery was successful and after the chemotherapy John was in complete remission. In no time, he was back to being his usual fun loving self. He was healthy, and happy with a new outlook on life. He returned to work with a head full of beautiful hair, it was a blessing. God still does miracles today!

Slipping back …

Life was great until one day John appeared to slip back into isolation, his disposition changed and the light in his beautiful eyes darkened. He was angry all the time because certain checks and balances were put in place to support the rehab process. He had limited access to our bank accounts and his pay check and this made him mad. He needed a fix and I was standing in the way. He picked an argument with me one day that didn't make any sense. He approached with violence in his eyes as he pushed me to the floor. He took our son Deavereaux, who was around 1 ½ years old, and threw him on top of me. Dev cried in hysterics, even as an infant he realized something was terribly wrong with Daddy.

John screamed, "You think you're so perfect! You're a bitch like any other bitch!" I realized this wasn't the man I married and had loved for so long. As the argument escalated, the police came to our home and took him away. By the time he returned I called my cousin to help move my belongings. I knew I had to go. I was so angry this was the thanks I received for being a loving and supportive wife.

I moved temporarily to my mom's house for about two weeks. Then Deavereaux and I moved to begin our life together. From this point, I chose to go it alone. I put all my energy into work and my son. I was a sports mom, as Deavereaux grew he played softball, soccer and my favorite, basketball. I loved him and he knew it. We would visit John from time to time within the first year of our break up. Then he moved out of state and we never saw him again. It was difficult raising Deavereaux as a single parent. I would have welcomed John's participation and support. Deavereaux missed his father immensely through the years. As time passed we had hoped that somehow a rekindling of a father son relationship would occur but unfortunately that day never came.

CHAPTER 4
Heart Skipping

Often my mind replayed many moments from the first season! It was our first time on the road. There was a knock at the door, for a second I thought it was my heart skipping a beat. The excitement of those first few games was overwhelming. It was a security guard ready to escort me over to the arena. I opened the door to a group of people who wanted to get a glimpse of the 'First African American Women to be General Manager and CEO of a Men's Basketball Team.' As the security guard walked beside me, men, women and children began to wave and nod their head in acknowledgement.

I was a little embarrassed because I didn't quite understand what all the fuss was about.

As time went on, I began to realize what an honor this was to be recognized as a 'First.' Being a 'First,' meant I had the opportunity to open doors for others.

As I walked into the arena, the Head Coach from the other team reached to shake my hand, the General Manager also reached out to congratulate me on the team. I walked to our bench and was told two seats were reserved; for me and the team's number one fan 'Tyler.' I looked out on the floor and there were the Las Vegas Stars dressed in the white 'away' uniforms and matching Adidas shoes. The Stars were a picture of true professionalism, tall giants ready to show the basketball world what they were made of.

The game began and we won the tip off, the stars put the first two points on the board.

It was like poetry in motion, we actually began to go to work and by the half we were up by 10 points. The Locker Room was buzzing because 'The Las Vegas Stars' had actually become a team. It was no longer about the individual player no egos were in the place. We came to win and that we did! As we came back on the floor after the half; the Stars played smart, dominated the boards and became a force to be reckoned with. The Stars never looked back, it was on to Victory. As the Stars left the floor, they slapped high fives, knowing that they were on their way.

The dream that began in my father had been planted in my heart so many years ago. Now it was blossoming into a reality. As we left the forum, I knew we had raised the bar for the sports industry. The professional basketball arena had two levels, the NBA and the other leagues. I wanted to see the players and staff look, act and play as if they were as professional as the NBA from the transportation, to the hotels, to the airline sponsor to the national sponsor. My past experience allowed me to believe it was possible! I guess my 'never say never' attitude came from having a father who taught, "You can do anything!" I had worked for Jessie Jackson a few years prior and he taught me to believe, "I Can."

My vision and dream was to bring a team to Las Vegas that 'Vegas would embrace!"

I wanted to give athletes a fair opportunity to showcase their talents to the NBA and International Pro-teams as well. I had studied the structure of Pro-Sports for many years and though some players come into the pro-ranks the traditional way. Others come in by playing for the International Basketball League and other leagues that are available. In the past these leagues were not handled as professional as the Minor Leagues in Baseball, but now there was an opportunity.

After the game the Stars piled back on the bus and headed back to the hotel for a shower and some dinner. The next morning the team and coaching staff were up early ready for the team shoot around. Walking into the gym with a confident swagger, the Las Vegas Stars were determined to win the second game. And make the 'Phoenix

Flames' a two time loser in front of their home audience. By being a mother of two boys I was well acquainted with the hustle and flow of victory and defeat. My own sons were growing up in competitive sports it was like balancing two families, the Stars on the court and my boys off the court.

CHAPTER 5
Bundle of Joy, Loss of Trust

My wonderful sons have been my strength when I had none and my motivation for entering the sports industry as an Agent and a Team Owner. Let me bring you up to speed on how my son Tyler came into my life. As the years passed after my divorce my focus was on raising my son 'Dev," and working as a nurse. I worked night shift at Davies Medical Center, got off work and took Deavereaux to school. Then rested a bit and worked with a local home health agency during the day. I was dating but nothing serious, especially after I found out the man I was dating was actually dating another woman. I was angry and disappointed and couldn't seem to find a normal relationship. "Where were the loyal, dependable men like my father, Abraham?" I kept asking myself.

One day I was out with a friend and the cutest guy walked into the restaurant. There was something about him that intrigued me. He walked in with a woman who appeared to be his girlfriend or maybe just a friend. We shared a few glances and I left to go to work. Approximately three days later my girlfriend and I were talking, "Remember the cute guy at the restaurant. He came over and gave me his number and asked me to get it to you." "Really," I was surprised and not sure how to approach this situation.

After speaking to a few girlfriends who were more liberal with their dating, I decided to give him a call. We set a time to get together, he was actually very nice. As time passed our relationship grew. He was very thoughtful and caring, qualities I was looking for ever since my relationship with John. Everyone liked Randy he was fun and a good hearted person. We were good friends and then one day that changed. Randy used the L word, 'LOVE,' which totally took me by surprise. I remember telling my friend at the time, "Randy has that look in his eyes. I think he's going to ask me to marry him." My friend Maritza listed all the great qualities most women are looking for in a man. She said in a matter of fact tone, "He's nice, good looking, hardworking, has a good job, adores and cherishes you, who cares what color he is, he's a good man!" she screamed. Later that week, Randy asked me out to dinner, took me over to meet his family and then began to talk about our future. Before I knew it, he had asked me to marry him and I said, "Yes!"

Married but confused...

On March 23, 1990 I married a man by the name of Randy Larson. He was a good man but my heart had been wounded. I could only give so much. All my friends admired his love for me it was an unconditional love. But it was difficult for me to trust again. I loved him as much as my heart could give at the time. He was good to me, Tyler and Deavereaux, he loved his family and was a good provider.

We moved to an affluent area in Northern California, and lived on a golf course. I drove a luxury car and he drove a corvette but something still wasn't right. I loved and admired Randy for wanting to be a husband to me and a father to Deavereaux. I was married but discontent for reasons I didn't quite comprehend myself. Our marriage was quite interesting, his mom and dad accepted me and my family accepted him. It was a mixed marriage.

On our wedding day, we were married in front of 200 of our closest friends and family. I asked Karyn to be one of my brides maids. She was so happy to be honored by being in the wedding. Looking back I remember sitting on the porch at Karyn's house before I met Randy. I basically told her I wanted to marry again and find a great guy. She advised me to pray about it. So, I did and shortly there after I met Randy. God works in mysterious ways. As I noted earlier God brings people into our lives for specific purposes. I realize God brought

Randy into my life. He is the father of my beautiful son 'Tyler' and played an instrumental part in acquiring the Las Vegas Stars. Over the years Randy has been a tremendous support and I'm indebted to him because of his generosity and consistency in my life.

Entrepreneurial spirit …

During our marriage I was working as a nurse at San Ramon Medical and the Rehab Center. The entrepreneurial spirit hit. I invited one of my closest friends to join me in starting a business, thus, "Education Planning Associates," was born. We decided to place the business in an affluent area. It was an area similar to Beverly Hills but it was in Northern California. I had the bright idea of hiring teachers with their Masters and/or PhD's to tutor affluent children. We began to network and bring in clientele from the affluent businesses and residential communities.

In no time we had parents from everywhere who wanted their children to reap the benefits from high level tutoring. At first the business was going well but after time the business partnership began to dwindle and the trust factor fizzled out.

To say the least this scandal rocked my world again. As I look back on the whole incident and the demise of this booming established business it taught me a few lessons about business partners I want to pass on. First of all, find someone you can trust. Start with their history. "What's their track record? Do they have a history of mishandling money, dishonesty or corruption? Ask yourself if you could trust them with the business finances. Are they the type of person who would be honest with the profits and overhead expenses of the business? Does this person have integrity?" Everyone makes mistakes in their lives but look for patterns of repeating the same misguided decisions. Above all else look for someone with ethical values and gifts such as love, peace, patience, kindness, longsuffering, goodness, faithfulness, gentleness, and self control. (Galatians 5: 22) Business can be very trying especially if moral ethics are not shared.

Beautiful baby boy...

On the bright side, on December 31, 1991, Tyler Cole Larson was born. He was a beautiful baby boy that was so cuddly and loving. It was as if he was an angel come down from heaven, it seemed he knew his purpose as a tiny babe to make our lives brighter. He was our heart. I was overwhelmed with having two healthy, loving sons. The grandmas took shifts to assist in taking care of Tyler. Grandma Charlene, Randy's mom stayed for three weeks to assist me during the day while my mom helped in the evenings.

Who would have thought that 15 years later Tyler and Deavereaux would be an integral inspiration prompting me to become a sports agent and owner of a professional basketball team! Tyler sat on the bench next to the team elated to be associated with a pro basketball team while his older brother played on the court. I often teased them, "You're going to be like the Maloof brother's owners of the Sacramento Kings."

CHAPTER 6
Miracle for Christmas

When Tyler was 9 months old I was driving on Hwy 80 and the heater core exploded in my car, leaving 3rd degree burns on my feet and legs. As the car filled with smoke I instantly began to panic. I imagined the car was about to catch on fire or explode leaving me a deformed, scarred woman. Fears of dying pulsed through my veins I panicked turned on the hazard lights and proceeded to move over to the slower lanes. The cars around me began to slow down. I reached the lane closest to the shoulder of the road and the brakes malfunctioned. I pumped the brakes and still the car was rocketing out of control. "Get out of the car, get out of the car," an inner voice screamed.

I opened the door of the car and rolled onto the shoulder of the road. The car was moving about thirty miles per hour. I remember hitting the asphalt like a ton of bricks. The car was moving fast enough when I bailed to severely injury my back and neck. The last thing I remember were sounds of metal crunching and glass breaking as the car went head on with a tree. Scenes from my life flashed then everything went dark. I wasn't sure how long I was unconscious.

When I woke police and firemen were standing over my motionless body. I breathed a sigh of relief knowing I was in good hands. The ambulance attendants began asking questions, "What's your name? What happened?" Tears flooded from a sea of emotion I had a second chance, God had spared my life. Again the paramedics pried for information, "Can you move?" Still asking questions they rolled me onto a gurney. One paramedic addressed the burns on my legs, trying to survey the damage and applied cool packs to my scorched skin. Another busily started an I.V and fluids entered my vein. They whisked me away to the nearest hospital.

I was taken to the Emergency Room with third degree burns on my lower legs, with a few bumps and bruises and a very sore neck. I was treated and discharged late that evening. My head was pounding and felt as if it could crack off my spine and roll away. Having been a nurse for several years I knew something was wrong. I was referred to Dr Kennessey, a well-known doctor in Danville, California. After taking X-rays, he diagnosed severe whiplash from the impact caused by a reverse curvature in my neck. He ordered Physical Therapy and Chiropractic care. I was referred to Dr Newman, a Chiropractor from the San Ramon area who worked wonders. I believe he spared me from being on pain medications for the rest of my life. I slowly recuperated and remained in therapy for an entire year.

Stress and strain...

The stress and strain from my illness caused problems in my marriage. For the first time in my adult life I was financially dependent on someone. Even though Randy was great, I was angry! My life had suddenly gone down the drain. I could no longer be a nurse due to the back and neck injuries. My financial picture was bleak and I wasn't able to work for over a year. "I was going crazy!" I thought. Anyone who knows me knows I'm a total Type A personality, unable to sit still for a minute let alone an entire year! My friends started suggesting different projects to keep my mind occupied, after all I wasn't an invalid. I had my good days and bad, it was hard to determine what each new day would bring. The good days were really good and the bad were so ugly and painful I couldn't get out of bed.

During those days spent in bed I made phone calls. My mind raced to explore business opportunities despite the pain in my head and body. As my year of convalescence passed, I started a talent showcase similar to Star Search. People tried out and competed for top prizes. The final show was huge with over a thousand people in attendance with fifteen performers, and one lucky winner. I was exhausted feeling like I had over done it a little. The next morning I went to breakfast with the team, I offered to drop one of the staff members off at his home. As we sat in the car still excited about the success of the prior evening it happened. "What happened?" I was groggy.

"I don't know," he replied.

"Do you know what just happened to me?" I weakly inquired.

He looked like he had seen a ghost and panicked, "Do you feel okay? I think you had a seizure. You were talking one minute, then your eyes rolled back in your head and your body began to shake. How do you feel?"

"I feel a little weird, kind of drowsy," my reply was slurred. His voice reached hysterics, "You need to go to the hospital."

"Here we go again," I sighed in anguish.

He called an ambulance the sirens and flashing lights soon engulfed the car with a flurry of action and frantic questions. In Emergency, the doctors ran tests and found indeed I had a seizure. They prescribed seizure medications and sent me home. Within the next few days my condition worsened. Flu like symptoms pelted my frame with aches, nausea, fatigue and fever. One morning my Mom and a friend came by to check on me. When they arrived with one look they agreed, "You're going to the hospital." I was so weak and groggy they literally lifted me off of the bed.

No hope …

I was taken to San Ramon Medical and admitted to the hospital. I lost approximately two weeks of cognition in a coma without much hope of living. I woke up one day on the medical floor across from the Intensive Care Unit. The doctors assumed I might have Lupus or cancer. My kidneys were failing I had been on dialysis for three weeks. All this was ironic; the nurses taking care of me were my coworkers. Several days passed and the medical staff was perplexed with my case. I heard the doctors talking to my mother outside my door. "We're baffled all the tests are inconclusive. We're sorry Mrs. Levi but we're not sure what's going on with your daughter." As I lay motionless, my mother looked on with tears in her eyes. Being the strong women that she was, she continued to care for me as if I were the picture of health, her faith reigned supreme. She would come in and comb my hair, wash my face and she would sit hours just waiting for any sign of life.

It was Christmas time and beautiful white lights glistened from the trees outside my hospital window. Life looked so perfect outside but inside one of the greatest dramas was being played out, the battle between life and death. Most people were busy shopping, decorating their homes, attending church services and enjoying grand festivities. "How I wished to be a part of it all," I mused.

Karyn walked into my room and with a glimpse calculated the severity of what was becoming a hopeless prognosis. I read her shocked expression which she tried to cover with a warm smile. I realized she was instantly surprised at my frail frame and lifeless disposition. As a Registered Nurse and was accustomed to the likes of death invading the human body, recognizing its look and smell. She drew close and wrapped her arms around me. I had no strength to reciprocate but cracked a weak smile, our eyes locked.

Sounds from our childhood erupted; we listened entertained by the carefree laughter of innocence dancing in the sunlight. Two little ones playing without a care, so much time had eclipsed those hallowed moments. Words weren't necessary only the memories. We could read the others mind, "How could life turn so quickly?"

I was receiving another dialysis treatment, my blood pumped through the clear tubing appearing as dark red wine. The machine hummed with vibration, beeped sporadically and hissed in low vacuum tones, it was literally my mechanical life line. She slowly sank in a chair dodging the tubing between my bed and the dialysis machine. I could barely open my eyes let alone carry a conversation. She prayed while glancing at the machine and followed the tubing attached to a well-placed port on my chest.

God has the power...

Understanding my life and destiny were no longer in my control I began to reflect back on my life. I had always been successful in business, drove nice cars and lived in nice homes but none of this mattered now. Many people were praying and I believe the unity blasted heaven's doors and that's why I'm alive today. We all have a way of running our own affairs and trying to accomplish what we think is best. In reality, God is there waiting for us to look up and say, "I surrender! I've lived by my own strength and ambitions long enough, and what have I gained? Yes, there's been some success and blessings from above but too often the roads were laden with pain and heartache." Most of us need to reevaluate where we're headed. We need to humbly ask, "God what's your plan for my life?" We need to slow down and listen for the answer.

Time of release...

Yes, it was very bleak! The doctors decided to order a kidney biopsy before determining whether I needed a possible kidney transplant. My kidneys had completely stopped functioning. "Were they talking about me? Alexis Levi, a woman who had never been sick, except for the prior neck injuries and burns from the accident the year prior. "Was I going to live?" my mind questioned. After the kidney biopsy was performed, I had to lie flat for eight hours due to doctor's orders.

Later that day it was time for yet another dreaded treatment of dialysis. My body was completely stressed and depleted. I was unrecognizable. My life was withering away, a mere puff of smoke being blown away by an unknown culprit. The nurse came into the room; a coworker I had worked with many times. "How are you today, Alexis?" she was trying to sound upbeat. "Okay," I grunted weakly. She replied: "The doctor wants me to sit you up so you can eat something." She lifted the head of the hospital bed with its control.

As the head of the bed inched higher my heart began to race! It felt as if my heart was going to jump out of my chest. "Was I having a heart attack?" My mind raced calculating the possibilities. I was frantic, "My heart's exploding! Why is this happening? I don't want to die!" I started praying, "God I don't want to die, please let me see my sons grow into men?" Deavereaux was nine and Tyler almost two years old. Memories of my fatherless childhood added to the shearing pain in my chest. I grew up without one of my parents and that was one of the most difficult challenges and didn't want that for my sons.

"Calm down," the nurse urged and called the doctor. He instructed her to give me a 1000 cc's of normal saline solution through an IV. "God if this is my time, I'm ready to see you." I was exhausted, weighing 120 lbs, 5ft 9inches. My heart continued to race, my chest was pounding and the piercing pain only intensified. In a twinkling the whole world with all its cares and concerns was left behind, fading into the background with all its noise and interruptions. I was in a state where I relinquished all dreams, aspirations and burdens. It was a time of RELEASE, giving all my burdens to an unseen visitor that entered the room at my greatest hour of need. In the midst of labored breathing, suddenly an overwhelming peace possessed my whole being. I closed my eyes and saw a light at the end of a long tunnel. It seemed far away, unreachable, yet it was still visible, real and not my imagination. The light dimmed, a short period of time passed I resurfaced from being on the heights of an unknown place.

As the fluids pulsed through my system I began to feel better. The chest pain subsided and I felt a wave of wellness pulse through my whole being. I was flooded with peace and strength. Suddenly, I had the intense urge to go to the bathroom. "I have to use the restroom" I demanded. The nurse humored me, "You haven't urinated in three weeks. It's just your imagination." That's what happens to people when their kidney's shutdown they're not able to filter the fluids in their body.

It felt like my bladder was going to explode. Despite objections the nurse walked me to the bathroom. "You're too weak for this," she protested. I hit the pot and sat for a few minutes and felt a whoosh! I began to URINATE! We both began to cry, "Unbelievable," my coworker rejoiced. God touched my kidneys and body! It was a miracle! The doctors were glistening with excitement. They had no idea what happened. They were scratching and shaking their heads over the next few days as we celebrated normal lab tests. The other patients thought we were all crazy as we rejoiced every time I urinated. God still does miracles today!

There was no scientific explanation for what happened to me in December, 1993. I was discharged from the hospital on New Years Eve; I had originally attempted to get out on Christmas. Since the miracle happened just a few days before, the doctors didn't feel comfortable releasing me so soon because I had been so deathly ill.

One day I was so determined to get out I kept bugging the nurses to contact Dr. Kennessey. "He's busy seeing patients said the head nurse. We've left messages, just relax and build your strength." My mischievous side came out, determined to get my way I called information and asked for his office number. "Hello, may I help you," the operator asked. "Yes, Dr. Kennessey in Danville, please?" "I'll connect you," she replied. The receptionist answered, "Dr. Kennessey's office." I disguised my voice as a nurse from San Ramon Medical. "I have an important message for the doctor regarding his patient Alexis Levi." "One moment I'll connect you," the receptionist muttered.

"Hello, this is Dr. Kennessey is everything okay?"

"Yes, this is Alexis Levi and I want to know when the discharge process will begin? I've been here almost a month and feel fine. I want to be home with my kids on Christmas!" Dr Kennessey explained, "Alexis, you were critically ill only a few days ago. Give us time to evaluate your progress. You're condition has dramatically improved but let me control when you go home." He was a bit agitated but sympathetic.

"I understand but I've never been away from my kids on Christmas," I pleaded.

Lex Is Back...

I woke up Christmas morning feeling well enough to regret not being home. "Cheer up," I thought. "Thank you God I'm alive and growing stronger by the minute." I asked the nurses to clean me up, curl my hair and assist me in putting on some makeup. If I was going to be in the hospital I wasn't going to look sick. The phone rang and my girlfriend Renee was on the line. "What's up chick? So, you finally decided to get it together? Lex is back?" she joked. We both began to laugh. "I'm coming over to see you." Renee avoided visiting it was difficult for friends and family to see me so lifeless. From the time Renee came to the time she left we laughed, talked, cried and then laughed again. It was the best Christmas gift ever! She came into the room and treated me as if I was the 'Lex' she had always known and loved. The laughter we shared gave me the extra fight I needed to make it through. We were like a couple of teenage girls!

The Physical Therapist came to the room to provide me my daily therapy. I had to learn to walk again as I once did when I was a toddler, I had become very weak from lying in the bed for almost a month. She asked, "Are you ready to show Renee what you can do?"

"Yes."

I put my robe on and we walked slowly around the entire floor. Day by day, I was getting better and before I knew it I was able to walk the entire length of the floor without getting tired. Later that day, my mom brought my sons to see me for Christmas. It was the best Christmas ever! We had no time for shopping and preparing a huge Christmas meal. It was then I realized the best gift God can give is life and your family. God still does miracles today!

CHAPTER 7
The Stalker

After I was discharge I realized my life would never be the same. Due to my history of neck injuries I was advised to give up nursing in order to prevent any possible future harm to my spine. I followed doctor's orders, my career was stripped away. "What would I do?" Unfortunately, all my medical problems caused a severe strain in my relationship with Randy. My injuries and convalescence contributed to the break up of our marriage. It was over and we would now go our separate ways. I don't condone divorce, experiencing the trauma and emotional pain going through it once is enough for anyone to endure. Truly, it is a tearing of lives and families sometimes it's justified and other times seemingly convenient, despite the long term consequences.

My so called admirer...

One of my business associates who come to the hospital at times began to come around more and more. He was a friend but there seemed to be an attraction on his part so this concerned me. He offered to take me and the kids to a friend's house for New Year's Eve. December 31st was the birthday of my youngest son Tyler it was truly a celebration of life and birth. Eventually, as time passed when I needed help my friend was always there. In time I began to depend on him. He offered gym training and I grew stronger. I was always slender, but I began to have curves that surprised even me. After a short time my body sculpted into a great physique. As the months passed I began to really feel good about myself.

One night my friend asked me to attend a bodybuilding competition. I said, "Sure." So I rushed home from work to get dressed. I showered and dressed and made my grand entrance into the living room. He looked me up and down and commented on my outfit, "Where are you going in that outfit?" "What's wrong, does it look bad?" I was concerned. "No, you look too good to be going out in that." "I'll be on your arm!" I smiled. His face strained with anger, "Take it off."

"Excuse me, I like you, but no one tells me what to wear. I'm a grown woman and my own family doesn't tell me what to wear." I turned away for a moment and when I looked back his fist hit me with a shattering blow. I lost consciousness for a while, blood spattered the room. My nose was broken! The facial pain was excruciating.

Feeling light headed and mad as hell I ran to the phone, he grabbed it from me. He immediately poured apologies, giving excuses for the violent, insane behavior, but it was too late. My cousin and my son were downstairs and I ran for safety. My so called friend escaped out the door. I pressed charges but for some unknown reason, nothing ever came of it. When I inquired at the police department I was told, "You came in and dropped the charges." "Wow, I never did such a thing," I complained and left the station wondering how such a blatant mistake could take place. On the night of the assault my attacker left apparently a free man. I never wanted to see him again.

Unfortunately, one day a few months later the inevitable happened. While driving down the street I came to a stop sign. He came out of no where and jumped into the passenger side of my unlocked car. He burst through with such force, I screamed in disbelief to see my tormentor 'face to face.' His eyes glared with wild anger and intent to harm. "Keep driving or I'll kill you," he hissed. I remained silent, calculating my words in order to prevent another bloody scene. I realized he was more than capable of following through on his threats. He forced me to drive for hours; finally he signaled me to pull into a Bart parking lot.

He continued rambling with bizarre statements, babbling nonsense, accusations, name calling and belittling, insinuating my behavior warranted his fist to break my nose. "I didn't want to hit you but you drove me to it," his words lashed in harsh criticism. His eyes flashed and darted looking to and fro not wanting any one to interrupt the perverted interrogation.

I was a hostage and my heart reeled in shock and unbelief. "Was he going to rape and then kill me after all the verbal abuse?" My mind questioned the possible out comes. I was kidnapped by a man who I thought was out of my life. He acted insane, irrational, and full of rage and I was his target. "What were his intentions in this secluded parking lot?" My mind raced thinking the worst, "I had just escaped from a near death experience, why was I being faced with another one? Eventually, a police officer approached the car, "Is everything okay?" Not knowing if my tormentor had a gun I motioned with my eyes, "I was not okay." The officer stepped around the car and confronted my oppressor, "I'm going to ask you to step out of the car and place your hands behind your head?"

I neglected to tell the officer about the kidnapping accounting it to nerves and severe panic. The officer put my oppressor on a Bart train home. Scared to death, I placed a restraining order against him the next day. Sometime later I got a phone call from him, "Alexis, we need to talk." I hung up the phone. He repeatedly left messages on my voicemail from 4 pm till the next morning around 7:00 am. The messages started out in a congenial tone but then ended in raging, threatening screams. The next morning my nerves were frazzled as I drove to my mom's house to drop off Tyler and pick up Deavereaux for church.

As it turned out, the stalker was waiting in my mother's garage. As I was leaving the house to get into my car, I was approached from the passenger side. He attempted to get in the car and take the keys. I jumped out of the car only to be tackled on the grass. His hands clasped my neck with a death choke hold. I was stronger now and began to fight back kicking wildly. He grabbed my hair and screamed, "Why are you hurting me? Why don't you want to marry me?" He methodically attempted to bang my skull on the cement. I kicked him in the groin and escaping his grasp ran into the back yard. By this time, my mom came outside screaming wildly, "Get your hands off of her you maniac. Leave her alone."

My son Deavereaux picked up the phone and called 911. Before I knew it there were four sheriff cars in front of my mom's house. One sheriff came through the side gate, two trailed him. "Are you okay," they asked. "No, he tried to kill me," I responded bleeding, with hair tossed, and ripped clothing. My head was spinning from the adrenalin rush and previous pounding. The officer asked, "Do you want to press charges?"

"Yes, but only if you promise me you're going to take him to jail. I pressed charges when he broke my nose and mysteriously the charges were dropped from the system."

My stalker looked at me with distain and a haunting smirk enveloped his face. The officers handcuffed him and sat him in the back of the police car.

"We'll make sure the charges stick this time." I never saw my so called admirer, turned stalker again.

"What did I learn from the whole nightmare?" For one thing especially for women we need to be very careful who we allow in our lives. Get to know a person's background, friends, and family. Ask seemingly innocent questions such as, "In your opinion does this person have an anger management problem? Have they ever been accused of any out of line behavior towards family members, ex-partners, spouses or even animals?" The answer to these questions could have saved a whole lot of drama.

When a person makes it to 'celebrity status' you never know what they've been through on the journey. Despite the hard road don't give up or think it's too late to live your vision and dreams. Each adversity is just a stepping stone to the path God wants you to take. As I look back over the last few chapters of turmoil, I realized I had to go through some of these changes in order to reach where I am today. My 'test' became my testimony. All the 'mess' became my message.

CHAPTER 8
The Boardroom

My personal life was in turmoil. "Without nursing what would I do?" I won the case against the dealership and they were forced to address the defect to the heater core. I was relieved other people would be spared so much potential harm and loss. After a long process of soul searching, I decided to go back to school and earn a 'Master's in Business Administration.' Being a business woman and entrepreneur had always been a goal of mine especially because my father was a business man.

I started looking for business opportunities and called the Oakland Chamber of Commerce. I happened to speak with 'Admiral Toney' on the phone; he was the President/CEO of the Oakland Metropolitan Chamber of Commerce. After explaining the recent occurrences in my life he replied, "The best avenue to get into the "Business World," is through the chamber. He immediately stated, a Sales Position was available, I interviewed and got the job. So I decided to take it. One of my gifts was communicating with people so I thought this would be a good opportunity.

Before long a position as a Sales/Marketing Manager opened. I had a good friend who worked for the chamber for a long time. So I asked her if she was going to apply for the position. "No," she replied. I put my resume in and got the job. It was my duty to interact with all the businesses in the 'City of Oakland' as well as any business wanting to come into the area. One of my responsibilities was to manage the sales staff and oversee the Chamber's events and business development, The job was demanding, I loved it because it catapulted me into the business world and was a vehicle in sharpening skills in sales, networking and business management. I completed my MBA over the next few years which ensured many tools for success.

Before long I was asked to attend, "The Boardroom," meetings on a regular basis. The most exciting account I brought to Oakland was the 'Raiders' football team when they returned to Oakland from Los Angeles. It was my department that worked with the City Officials to launch a citywide party to celebrate their return.

I learned the "Boardroom," can be filled with drama and laughter. Many times it was unclear what course a board meeting would take it all depended on the issues and finances involved. I've seen grown men laugh, cry and swear like sailors when crossed. Boardrooms are also places of competition in a different arena, when hundreds of thousands or millions are involved the sharks can come in for a kill. Positions and titles are at stake, and every word weighed and counted. Boardrooms can be a treacherous place in a person's career but the education and experience was priceless.

A few years passed and I continued battling it out in the "Boardroom." The issues varied, opponents on both sides had the capacity to devour each other, friends one moment and enemies the next. Quaint conversations moments earlier could quickly spiral into sly remarks, criticisms, outlandish put downs, and mocking jokes. The Board Room is an interesting place and it prepared me for the locker room and the world of professional sports politics.

The 'Boardroom' toughened my character and sharpened my business sense. I found it a major tool in defining a savvy business sense. It seemed the same for all industries, a certain serious gesture takes place when the cherry wood door closes and the stone faces begin to discuss the opposition.

Opportunity knocks…

Time passed, and one day I was at Tyler's school which just happened to be the preschool where I attended with Karyn. "Where did the years go?" Is a very nice woman who I would later come to know as the mother of Famous Rap Artist E-40. As we built a relationship, she introduced me to her daughter SUGA-T, and son D-Shot, Donell Stevens and Mugzi Delon Stevens. At the time, their new album had gone gold and it vastly climbing toward platinum status. It was truly an exciting time. One day, E-40 asked me to work for his corporation and to manage his sister, Suga-T, and the rest is history. I would sometimes tour with E-40 and Suga-T, this experience introduced me to the Grammys, Awards Shows, TV Networks, and Major Record Label executives.

On one occasion Suga-T and I attended the Magic Show in Las Vegas, a very high profile trade show for the fashion industry. We met several designers as well as a guy that worked for 'Stress Magazine.' He called her when we returned home and stated that MTV was looking for a girl rapper to join the cast of "The Lyricist Lounge". The Lyricist Lounge was similar to "Saturday Night Live," and "In Living Color." Rappers would come on and participate in the skits and rap the dialogue.

Because of her natural talent, and my shrewd negotiating, she was soon on her way to MTV Studios. She ended up staying for a whole season. Working within the music and television world has always been exciting. I was fortunate to travel and be a part of the music industry for over eight years. As time elapsed I eventually pursued my own career interests.

My own TV show...

I spent several years hosting my own show locally with Channel 19, a local Bay Area cable network. I was also a remote commentator with "In Depth Profile On Fox TV" an "Entertainment Magazine" style talk show working outside the studio. One of my favorite roles while commentating was interviewing celebrities such as Arnold Schwarzenegger, Sinbad, Tupac, Morris Chestnut, and Jermaine Dupree. I even had a short acting career in which I played E-40's mom in his documentary, "Charlie Hustle, A Self Made Millionaire."

Work ethics and Jessie Jackson...

At one point I was traveling more than once a month and away from my sons. A friend contacted me and told me of a position in Business Development that was available working with International Leader; Jesse Jackson. I was chosen out of 60 applicants. It was my job to interact with Corporate CEO's in the Silicon Valley Area, as well as business leaders nationwide. Diversity in the corporate workplace was my passion, qualified women and people of color deserved an opportunity to sit on the Corporate Board of Directors, and corporate contractors were also asked to think of a diverse marketplace.

Once again I was asked to interact with business leaders and corporate executives. I learned great skills in work ethics being around Reverend Jesse Jackson. I learned to be personable and treat everyone the same. He began calls at 3 - 4 am and then went to his room late in the evening after working 12-14 hour days. He always made sure his partners and strategic alliances were mutually benefited. He preached business ownership. I believe working with Reverend Jackson was the best job I had during my boardroom years. There were parties, celebrities, and conferences, the experience was phenomenal. The highlight of one of the conferences was an appearance by actor Chris Tucker, events with celebrities like Barbara Streisand and Corporate events with CEO's from the largest technology city Silicon Valley.

Pay2ViewTV...

I was always an idea person; I came up with an idea to have my own online TV Network. Thus, Pay2ViewTV was developed; it began with sports channels and grew into a 10 channel network. For two years, I worked with technology professionals to develop the website. After another two years we began to secure content. I'm still currently working on this project but recently changed the name to The HoTT SpoTT.

Life in the 'Boardroom' still continues today and the skills I acquired serve my business ventures daily.

Similarly, the 'Boardroom' hasn't been much different than life in the "Locker Room." Owning the 'Las Vegas Stars' plunged me into many difficult business situations and dealings specifically with hard nosed business men whose goal was winning! So, during certain disputes and discrepancies over the season it wasn't foreign when heads began to fly, ego's flared and power trips manifested. Thankfully, I was groomed by the corporate world of business that helped keep my wit and cool when the "Locker room," called. After all its daunting moments, the

"Boardroom," trained and equipped me for the International Basketball League and birthing the Las Vegas Stars.

Alexis as a little girl

Abraham Levi : Alexis Dad

For color photos, go to
alseg1.wix.com/alexislevi and
alseg1.wix.com/sportsforlifeusa

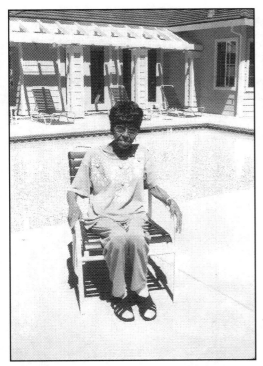

Gladys Levi : Mother

Deavereaux Oldest Son

Tyler Youngest Son

Tyler at Home

Stars Billboard

Alexis Levi and Karyn Schofield Darnell: Best Friends

Credit: Pepsi First of Many Ad Campaign
Black History Month 2008

CHAPTER 9
Love and Struggles

I was still looking to make my business Pay2ViewTV successful and to hopefully meet a man just like my 'Dad.' I dated a few good men but nothing serious had accumulated. I was working on my Internet project with my business associate, Bobby Gasper. We were still developing an online television network which took time and ingenuity. This all proved life consuming. I had decided to move to Redondo Beach in Los Angeles to pursue the dream of Entrepreneurship.

One day Tyler and I were driving down Lakeshore Avenue in Oakland and a familiar face pulled up next to me at the light. "Hey, how are you?" asked Pete. "Pullover I want to give you an invitation to my party," his voice bellowed over the traffic. I pulled over, we exchanged information. Pete was an acquaintance, we weren't close friends. He went on to say he was throwing a party and wanted to invite me and a couple of my friends to attend.

I invited Jackie and Mary to attend the party with me. So, as fate would have it, Jackie, Mary and I met in Oakland and caravanned to the party. As we drove up the street we found ourselves in the Oakland Hills. We parked and walked towards a splendid house. We met several other people walking towards the house who had also been invited to the party.

We stepped inside what appeared to be a mini mansion with exceptional decor. The guests glanced at us with approval. This was definitely the place to be. There was a nice layout of food and beverages.

One of the guys volunteered to bartend for the night. It felt good to be out relaxing for a change. I picked out this great leather outfit and felt like a million dollars. As we stood near one another, a very attractive gentleman addressed us, "Can I get you ladies something? My name is Marco."

I smiled, "Yes, I'd like a glass of wine." He promptly left to fill the order. My girlfriend said, "Oh, girl! I think he likes you."

"Girl please, I'm not in the market besides I'm moving to L.A. I don't have time for romance." I had plans and wanted to fulfill them all.

When he brought back the wine I detected a high level of interest. "Oh, God what's going on," I thought. He brought everyone drinks as well. The guests began to dance; I danced a few songs with other gentlemen. As I came off the dance floor, I noticed his eyes glued on me. We all disbursed for a minute, some to the food table, and others to the restroom. Mary said, "I don't know what you did but he's inquiring about you." Sounding matter of fact I commented, "Do you see those pretty green eyes, tanned skin and muscles, that is nothing but trouble." My eyes shifted in his direction. Mary explained, "He's doing some work in the music media industry and seems really nice."

"Yeah, yeah," I said skeptically laughing all the while.

Words in action...

As the evening progressed we were having a great time. I was walking off the dance floor in the direction of my friends when Marco came out of no where, grabbed my hand and swooped me off to the dance floor. It must have been a testosterone rush, he didn't even ask me to dance. It was all body language, 'words in action' and a big grin. "What was his motive?" I thought while gazing into his green eyes. He was exceptionally handsome, but I was sure he was like all the others. I didn't need any more negative experiences with men. We talked a little and then I went back to hanging with my girls, he definitely was focused on getting to know me. I had to leave early because the next day Jackie and I were having a birthday party for her son and I was going to help. He and I exchanged numbers and that was the end of the meeting.

The next morning I awoke with a start the phone ringing became my alarm clock. I groped for the phone trying to focus, "Who could be calling me this early?" It was Marco! "Can I see you today?" he asked feverishly. I deviously answered, "Well, you can come to an eight year olds birthday party." My voice was still cracking trying to sound awake. I planned on unleashing my seven year old son Tyler on him and he'd soon be gone. He arrived and was introduced to Tyler immediately. I wanted to make sure Marco left early. I wanted to help with the party without distractions. Shortly, afterwards Tyler asked, "Can I go to the store with Marco?" So, much for my aversion strategy, I thought, "Wow, I guess he's alright!"

We began dating; he was like a dream come true. He had all the qualities I liked. He was nice, and liked my kids and they adored him. We got along great, I felt like it was really true love. We weathered all the storms as best friends and protected each other. We decided to get married if we were together a year and still felt such a strong connection.

The day came, we had a beautiful wedding with all our friends and family, it was one of the greatest days of my life. I felt so settled, Marco was such a gentleman. We combined my two sons with his son and became a family. All of our friends envied our relationship because there was no question, "We loved each other."

Distressing conflicts…Blackballed

Throughout our marriage, Marco and I dedicated our time to working in the music industry as agents and with the kids, supporting their sports ambitions. One day my son Deavereuax asked Marco and I to take him to a 3 on 3 basketball tournament, with his friend and one of his cousins. This game was to be held at Great America. We signed them up and away we went. At this time, Dev was fifteen years old, 6ft 4 inches tall and played with speed and agility. He had natural talent groomed over the years by playing on school and local church teams. The team secured second place with over 100 teams involved. The coaches and referees stopped and talked to us about Dev after seeing his performance and stature on the court. They were interested in him and one of the referees introduced him to the head coach at one of the local high schools.

As a freshman at Pinole high school, he tried out for the team but his grades were bad so he sat out a portion of the season. He was able to return when the grades improved but unfortunately the coaches didn't give him much playing time. He was discouraged because he had worked so hard to get his grades up. Dev was so excited to have another opportunity to play he couldn't wait for the call from the other school.

The coach called and talked to Deavereaux about transferring to this other local high school. Marco and I talked about it; this school was noted for having a tough reputation. It was located in the flat lands of Richmond, California one of the killing capitals in the nation. The first day of school Dev called, "I'm still alive." He laughed to tell me the kids named him, "Rich boy." We weren't rich but very fortunate in our lives. Dev was like a chip off the block, he got along with everyone just as I was raised to get along with all cultures and races. He was happy! This coach had an exemplary after school study program.

The head coach knew the game of basketball but he was verbally abusive. He'd curse at the kids, throw chairs and sometimes humiliate them. This unacceptable behavior happened over and over, I began keeping close tabs on the situation. He eventually targeted my son and I became furious this type of behavior had become so common place in all levels of sports. I ended up calling the Principals office after he appeared to constantly pick at Dev. After distressing conflicts with the coach, Dev decided to step down to Junior Varsity even though he was recruited for Varsity. He wanted to play but game after game he sat the bench for what reasons we don't know. Despite all his talent it seemed he was being overlooked, blackballed and purposely set aside. So, without much raucous Dev stepped down from Varsity and was happy to play for Junior Varsity, as long as he played.

The situation on the J.V. team became unbearable when athletes with less talent were played ahead of Dev. We found out the Varsity Head Coach began to manipulate the J.V coaches to prevent Dev from playing even on the J.V level. "Why was Dev being blackballed? Was it because I contacted the authorities? I guess this was the coach's way of getting revenge," I contemplated the disheartening situation. "Why was my son being treated so miserably?"

I contacted the Principal, the Mayor (whom was a friend of the family) and the Governor. It was crazy, other parents just stood by while their kids were belittled, humiliated, and cursed with chairs continuing to fly across gym floors. "What was this behavior teaching the students about sports conduct and life in general? Is this how frustrations are handled?" I mused. "What type of coaching example was this for these young men?" I continued to question. The more I thought about it the more it erupted and fumed as something to be addressed not only at the high school level but on all levels of the sports world. This whole scenario was preparing me to lead the Stars in the future.

The day after I contacted the Mayor and Governor I found out the head coach at this High School resigned and sent a letter to the local newspaper. Apparently, he was angry his behavior and conduct were being called into review. I thought, "Why does having the title of "Coach" or "Manager" suddenly give rights to abuse athletes with manipulation, fear tactics, verbal abuse and control?" It's amazing to see how coaches and managers can use these titles to manipulate an athlete's life and future for the good or bad. I understand athletes can have problems, attitudes and egos of their own and coaches and managers put up with a lot also. However, for the most part I've seen the scales tipped towards coach and management misconduct more than athletes being the problem.

I can tell you countless stories of coaches helping athletes go on to earn scholarships to major universities, or go 'pro' which is so commendable. On the other hand, there are coaches who for reasons of their own have failed to give athletes 'letters of interest' from major universities or failed to help athletes move forward despite their talent.

Many athletes are sabotaged in order to block possible advancement. Sometimes it has to do with 'egos and personality conflicts.' Regardless, on all levels I feel coaches need to be supportive and not a hindrance. I'm passionate about basketball and felt concerned about the misguided behavior of this particular coach that's why I was compelled to do something about it.

Full ride scholarship...

One day Dev had a tournament at Marin Catholic high school in San Rafael. Marco and I were pretty intense; we would talk to Dev before the games to keep him focused and on the task at hand. Scoring and rebounding in the double digits, he was headed for a college scholarship. Because of his long stature 6ft 5" and special coordination, he had a special way of leaping and grabbing the ball right off the rim.

At the tournament as Dev was going down the court, I waited for his coach to give him instructions; before I knew it I proceeded to run down the sideline giving my coaching instructions. Now, most coaches hate to see parents interfere at this level, but truly, I knew what I was doing. One day I decided to pay Dev ten dollars per dunk. I began to go broke. It was common for him to have 2-3 dunks in a game. We all laughed as I handed more and more money over to Dev.

Life was moving forward Dev graduated from high school and earned a GPA of 3.0 for his last semester grades. He landed a full ride scholarship to Lower Columbia College, a Junior College in the Portland Oregon area. School was never easy for Dev, he was always cautious about his grades. We as a family believed in his ability and his positive attitude. So, we encouraged studies and sports. After one year at Lower Columbia he returned for the summer and began working out with two trainers Lou Ritchie and Jesse McGaffee.

Several colleges began looking at Dev but he decided to stay in California which meant he had to complete his AA degree or close to it before transferring over to a four year college. He attended Merritt College to complete his AA degree. He played basketball for the college and ended the season the top scorer on the team. Dev received several calls from universities all around the United States. He was almost ready to commit to Chaminade University, Hawaii.

"Are you excited about the possibilities at Chaminade?" I asked.

"Mom, it's a ways from home; will the family come and visit?" he answered.

"If you had your choice, where would you like to go?"

"Clark Atlanta University," he blushed.

I called Clark Atlantic's athletic department and told the coach about Deavereaux and his abilities. The coach asked me to send transcripts, a video tape and to have Dev give him a call. As things worked out, 'Clark Atlanta University Athletic Department' called and gave him an opportunity. We were so excited. He received a scholarship to attend the school so off he went.

My mind kept returning to all the difficult incidences Dev had with some of his coaches on the high school level. The opportunity for college scholarships would have been ruined if this coach's behavior was unchecked. I still shudder to think what would have happened to so many of his team mates mentally and emotionally if future scholarship opportunities were methodically denied for unknown reasons. Fortunately, better, fairer coaches stepped in and changed the course of 'scholarship opportunities' for many on the team. Dev went on from Clark Atlanta to even greater opportunities and played exhibition games for the Las Vegas Stars.

Music Industry...Family ...

Time rolled on as our lives played out, Marco was completely immersed in the fast paced lifestyle of the music industry which was not conducive to family life in the long run. Eventually, this caused a lot of problems in our household. It soon became all about the studio, and the artists. Unfortunately, family priorities were last on the list. Marco and I became the hottest management team in Northern California for awhile. He made the connections; I handled the paperwork and did the negotiations. We were a great team! Before long artists were calling from everywhere! Despite, booming success the music business began to come between us, the late nights, the late nights and the disrespect came to the forefront. Through it all I continued to work full time besides handling the music business and tried to keep the family together.

Eventually troubled waters engulfed our relationship, our family failure was evident. There were so many signs that our marriage was in deep trouble. I was in denial until one day a heard a still small voice, "Go, look in his coat pocket." I never searched his clothing so I felt guilty for even having the thought. The voice kept repeating itself. At first I looked in his outer pockets and then closed the closet door. The voice said, "Keep looking." I went back and then searched the inner pockets and found a cluster of condoms. I instantly began to tremble as tears rolled down my cheeks.

It was our anniversary; what a way to celebrate. My cell phone rang, it was Marco. My heart sank to hear his voice. I loved and trusted this man. He was my husband, coworker and confidant, we shared everything in life. "Where are you?" he asked somewhat annoyed. "I'm at home, I'll be right there," my voice quivered. I fought back the tears refusing to admit the betrayal. We were scheduled to meet friends for dinner to celebrate love and marriage. "What a mockery of God's plan," I thought leaving the house and crying the entire way, still clutching the condoms in one hand, driving with the other. I realized it was happening again the demise of another relationship. "Was I so blind not to see all the signs, the late nights, and inattention?" my mind raced. Truly, God was trying to show me what I wanted so desperately to ignore. I wanted this marriage to work, my heart was broken.

Pulling up to the restaurant I called from my cell and asked Marco to come to the car. I couldn't possibly sit through an anniversary dinner without crying. "Yes," he said, somewhat irritated. "I have something to talk to you about," I tried not to let my emotions influence the sound of my voice. As he sat down in the passenger seat and closed the door I threw the cluster of condoms on his lap! "How could you? I trusted you!" I screamed. We instantly began to argue and as most men do he tried to explain his way out of it. He scrambled for any explanation that wouldn't incriminate him! Although I had not actually caught him with another woman and he never admitted to it committing adultery, this instantly ruined our marriage; once the trust was gone there wasn't a whole lot to hold onto. I was on the rebound, hurting, and emotionally torn and tattered. As the months lapsed, Marco and I were distant strangers living under the same roof. We tried counseling but it became apparent hidden games were played. The restoration of our marriage seemed elusive.

One night I was out with my girlfriends and met a very handsome man. He and I had great chemistry; we were instantly attracted to one another. I had so much hurt in my heart it made it easy for me to fall into another mans hands. He began to call me all the time, I began to sneak out and meet him. As soon as Marco would leave, I'd go out to meet him. It was crazy, it was wrong. I was desperate and misguided all at the same time. From this point forward things would never be the same, though we didn't sleep together, I was still in a bad place and tried to justify this emotional affair, " "Was I any better than Marco who had obviously given up on our marriage? I had to admit I committed emotional adultery." We needed to forgive each other, but that was easier said than done. I guess I pointed the finger at Marco and all the others who betrayed my trust, love and life.

Life Check... Inventory...

Over the following months I decided it was time for a life check. You know when you sit down in a quiet place and really have it out with yourself. It was time to take inventory on my own life, attitudes and behaviors which affected my marriage and family relationships. I had to admit, at times I can be demanding, harsh, and driven. In the past I have expected spouses and business associates to be goal oriented, and driven. When this wasn't the case I was disappointed and wasn't shy about my feelings. We all have the capacity to say mean, harsh, belittling things especially to those we love the most, our spouses, children, relatives and coworkers.

I've learned ways to communicate and empathize with others and draw closer to God through all the positive and negative experiences. The goal is to treat people with the golden rule, "Do to others as you would have them do to you." My focus in the last few years hopefully has shifted and matured to not necessarily having it all but being my best. I'd like to think I'll be able to provide for my family plus influence others in a positive light.

The relationship between Marco and I continued to dwindle. Sometimes I think we only stayed together for convenience. I loved him but we were growing apart, one suspicious event after another proved to me that the trust and loving connection that is supposed to be present in a marriage was no longer there.

Different men were interested in dating me; I traveled a lot with my job and interacted with businessmen from all around the world. To tell you the truth, I loved my husband and didn't even really notice these men. When on the road, I couldn't wait to get home to my family. My whole mindset was working hard so my family and I could enjoy nice things. It appeared Marco and I moved on different tracks. He was chasing the music business and all that went with it, wine, women and song.

The day I finally left the situation was one of the most hurtful days in my life. I wanted to be married and enjoy my family. Marco and I had always yearned for success and we had plans of growing old together. But out of respect for myself, I had to go! He needed to find what he felt was missing in his personal life and I needed to find what I believed was a better situation in life. In November 2006, we split. Marco went his way and Tyler and I went ours.

Once again the wind of change was on the horizon, the sail boat of life was changing directions. It had been about thirteen years since God healed me. I had the privilege of seeing my oldest son grow into a fine young man of twenty-two. Tyler was fifteen years old. My prayers were chronologically being answered. My sons were men in training. Time was ebbing away carrying me into uncharted waters. Everything was changing.

The LOCKER ROOM was calling.

Uncertainty...

I was a single parent again and fought feelings of abandonment and uncertainty about many circumstances in life. I was once again burdened with taking on the responsibility of being head of household. At times it all seemed so foreboding and burdensome. "Where was life going?" My days raged on like a battle ground, something was always upside down. Life was never short of problems and multiple demands stretched me so thin I feared being 'torn to threads' by circumstance.

If all this stress wasn't enough my elderly mother became ill; dementia appeared to be setting in. One day the management from the senior complex called, "Your mother's more confused." The neighbors complained she was setting off the fire alarm when preparing food. She'd put something on the stove and move to the next task. The kitchen would fill with smoke and trip the fire alarm. She was becoming a danger to herself and others. "What was I going to do?" Being an only child and a single parent struggling to survive stretched my available time and energy. I added a second job to already working a full time position. I worked in the mortgage industry with Wells Fargo and I had a second job at a High Profile Public Company down in the Silicon Valley area. I was trying to make as much money as possible to secure my new venture, 'The Las Vegas Stars.'

My daily routine was as follows: Up at 5:30 am, take Tyler to school, commute one hour, work day; 8-12 hours, quitting time, drove almost 1 1/2 hours through traffic to pick Tyler up in Vallejo where we lived. Then we proceeded to Concord where Mom lived, cooked dinner, cleaned the kitchen, and helped Tyler with homework. After all this I found myself falling asleep on mom's couch trying to catch up on needed sleep. The next day the same routine recycled all over again. I was literally exhausted.

CHAPTER 10
New Beginnings

Though life seemed like a snow flurry of frantic mundane and habitual business. At times I reminisced on what life had been with my son's and Marco. One particular evening replayed in my mind like a late night rerun, over and over. Before Marco and I split up Deavereaux and several of his friends were at the house. Our house seemed to be a gathering place for all the friends. Marco and I would cook and make them feel at home.

This particular night each began to recall negative coaching experiences on the high school and college level in the sports area. We laughed as I talked about how it was back in the day! I humored them in an almost bragging voice, "My coach was my best friend, always encouraging me to do my best, never belittling or humiliating. My coaches were always uplifting and pushing me to strive for peak performance. Never cussing me out or embarrassing me in front of people or my teammates." They were amazed that coaches were expected to be an example of positive sportsmanship. They said, "We felt like numbers instead of athletes."

As a result Dev and his friends begged me to start my own team. "We want you to be our coach," their voices whined in unison. We joked about the possibility, "Imagine me as your coach." My heart sank hearing one horror story after the other about misguided coaches who used their so called power to intimidate, ridicule, and sabotage. "So many games, so much drama," they complained. They spoke of the politics and how it ruined the excitement of playing sports for many athletes.

Kairos Time...

That evening proved to be another God appointed moment, a Kairos time in life. As a result I was motivated to help protect the future for my sons in the sports world. As a result in 2005 I became a 'Sports Agent Advisor' with Sports Management Worldwide. As a Sports Agent I was trained in negotiations and the politics of the professional sports world. It became apparent beginning in 2004 that coaches were recognizing Dev as a potential college and professional basketball player. I wanted to be prepared for the negotiation process for both Dev and Tyler in the days to come.

Eventually, Sports Management Worldwide began referring athletes to me for sports management. As a Sports Agent Advisor, I heard all the war stories athletes around the world were experiencing in the politics of professional sports. It was an honor to represent athlete's and fight for the best opportunities for them. After all their futures were at stake and I wanted to help them secure the best outcome.

A few years after Dev left for Clark Atlanta University unconsciously with no real motive, I began to do some research about teams and found a list of leagues such as the International Basketball League (IBL), American Basketball Association (ABA), Continental Basketball Association (CBA), National Basketball Development League (NBDL) and the World Basketball Association (WBA). Watch out, radical brainstorming started computing, "What would it be like if I owned my own team? Would I be fair to the players?" My mind filtered the possibilities and I began to look at the criteria for owning a team.

The brain storming followed with a mind track of research, investigation and then planning. I eventually decided to inquire about the process of owning a team with the International Basketball League. I spoke to the commissioner of the league about the pros and cons of placing a team in Las Vegas, Nevada. When he heard how serious I was about placing a team in Las Vegas, he decided to fly to the Bay Area. I pulled together some potential partners on the project and we met to discuss the options, the negotiations began. Upon completion of the negotiations, we set off to begin making arrangements for the press date. There we were at the Tarkanian Center making a "Press Announcement," about our plans to have a team in Las Vegas, Nevada.

Unbelievably, after the press conference something unplanned happened, 'story of my life.' A dividing spirit among the ownership group developed. The newly formed ownership team was now at odds and began bickering in agitation. Discussions and financial arrangements were made but suddenly one of the four partners pulled out. Once the primary partner pulled out I was told an exorbitant amount of money in three days was required on my part. This proved the first of many challenges ahead. "How would I come up with so much money by myself?"

I was being threatened off the ownership team because of last minute financial pressures. I always say there is 'no friendship in money and power.' Incredibly I was able to pull my portion of the deal together through others who were willing to invest. One day I received a call from the partners stating they no longer wanted Las Vegas; they only wanted St. George, Utah. I countered with the desire to own a team in Las Vegas for obvious reasons. I loved Las Vegas and felt it was the place to manage a team but the commissioner would have to approve the decision. Shortly after I received a call from the commissioner, we had a long conversation, one that would change my life forever. He said, "You want Las Vegas; I really think you can do it by yourself." I agreed and became the owner of the Las Vegas Stars. I didn't know whether to cry or laugh. At first, it really didn't sink in; Alexis Levi owned a men's professional basketball team in Las Vegas. Suddenly my mind began to swirl with plans and ideas. "How I was going to make this the best team in the International Basketball League?" My goal was to elevate the visibility of the IBL. I envisioned in five years, I could grow the Las Vegas Stars to be a household name worldwide.

Accolades and interview offers poured in. One day I received a call from Hernando Pernal, NBA Scout stating he wanted to take a look at our team. Another day, I received a call from Alzea Calhoun with the Cleveland Cavs who wanted to take a look at our players. This had to be a dream. I then received a call from Sean Higgins eight year veteran of the NBA. He was back in town from playing with the Continental Basketball Association and was interested in helping with the coaching and getting some playing time.

Time pushed forward, it was imperative I had to choose a Head Coach. It was recommended I hire a coach with experience so we did. We called him GT for short and he had years of experience in the basketball industry. I called GT, talked to him about the team, my dreams, and aspirations. I was thankful he joined the Stars as the coach. I'll never forget the day of our first tryouts. I walked in with a Las Vegas Stars t-shirt on, 5 ft 9in, looking more like a cheerleader than the owner of a professional basketball team.

GT was very friendly but I could read his mind he didn't quite know what to make of the situation. The players arrived and signed up for the try outs. They began shooting around, some stretching on the sidelines, a few others running laps. Excitement was in the air, the clock was on countdown mode, it was five minutes before tryouts for the LV Stars. The time clock sounded. GT and I walked to the center of the floor. We welcomed the first twenty guys. "Thank you for attending the first of the Las Vegas Stars tryouts! I'm Alexis Levi, Owner, CEO and General Manager for the Las Vegas Stars. The instructions for the day will be provided by the head coach."

When Coach GT stepped forward to speak his presence demanded respect. He and his family represented a living trophy in the world of basketball. He symbolized victory and success in this arena. He began with providing his expectations and instructions to the, would be, hopefuls. He held a clip board in his hands and began barking authoritative orders and instructions. Immediately the athletes were plunged into a rigorous routine that would change some of their lives forever. As instructed the athletes began performing jump shots, slam dunks, shooting drills, and ordered offensive and defensive exercises.

GT knew what he was looking for and keenly observed all the players while making mental notes of the strengths and weaknesses in each player. About midway GT asked, "Who do you see out there?" I realized this was a test question; would I pass? I instantly began to run down the strengths and weaknesses of each player. GT smiled, as if to say, "You do know basketball." GT and Higgins didn't realize I was keeping a little secret from them who stood about six foot, eight inches tall, a tower of bronze and strength, who at one time was carried under my heart for nine months.

My son Deavereaux had been playing with Clark Atlanta wanted to try out for the Las Vegas Stars to my surprise. I begged him at first to come to the LV Stars in the second year because I knew the first year would be a rollercoaster of unexpected events and tides of unknown adventure and challenge. He demanded, "It's something I have to do." His desire was so compelling, "Come on Mom," he pushed. I told him if he came he wouldn't be paid. "Then, you have to try out like anyone else," I demanded.

After many heated discussions, I sent him an airline ticket. We kept our secret from the other athletes as well for the try out period. He arrived in Las Vegas, was picked up by a limousine at the airport and transported to the Palace Station Hotel. Dev was athletic and ready to play and instantly gelled with Coach GT. He was young, twenty two years old, very impressionable, and eager to make it happen. During the try outs it was difficult to hide my emotions when I saw Dev doing so well. I wanted to start cheerleading, "Give me a "D," give me an "E," give me a "V," go DEV." I purposely curbed my smiles. Towards the end of the try outs I did get in a few words of praise for him. Then clapping my hands supposedly for all the players I knew who the praise was really for, my first born. Then giving him a big wink, without anyone noticing, our eyes made contact, a whole unspoken conversation transpired. We both knew it by instinct, he impressed GT and his name more than likely would be on the roster tomorrow.

We held approximately four tryouts including seventy five athletes before choosing the 2007 Las Vegas Stars. The end result was the following Roster: Hollis Hale, Deavereaux Vinzant, Sean Higgins, Dean Browne, Jason McGowan, Dajuan Tate, Eddie Shelby, Willie Hall, Trevor Lawrence, Matt Winans, Maurice Thomas, and Jonathan Walker.

Telling the world...

It was so hectic; I had to get the word out about this new venture. I sent out several press releases to the Las Vegas Press, only to receive little recognition. As I pulled on my past experience in marketing and business development I thought, "What is the one thing that gets the press excited? I got it! The National Press talking about something that is happening in your city!" I called Toni Beckham from PR Etcetera, an old friend of mine. I told her of my latest venture and asked her to help me write a press release. She instantly asked, "Think about it, are you the first African American woman to own a professional men's basketball team?" I shrugged my shoulders not really thinking along those lines. Her questioning continued like a semi automatic, "What's your title," I said, "Owner, CEO and General Manager." I surprised myself, "Wow."

We did some research and found no other 'African American woman' had purchased a Men's Professional team and held all three titles. This was a First! Toni began to write what would be the Press Release of the Year! The Press Release went out and within an hour Toni's phone was ringing off the hook! There were so many calls she couldn't handle it and found it difficult to get to her other clients. Toni was awesome we both soon learned this was bigger than the both of us. "I was making history!"

That afternoon I began doing interviews and the events haven't stopped. That evening I sat in my room and cried, "I had finally found my purpose, doing something I'm passionate about!" If we live out our lives only earning a pay check and neglect our talents, and true calling in life then we should be labeled the 'living dead.' So many of us forfeit being our authentic selves because we look at our circumstances and limit what God can do if we step out in Faith, you will be surprised what can happen.

This whole series of events and new beginnings was like an awakening for me in so many ways. Basketball was a joy and passion in my life, my whole family shared the sport. Not to mention my real motive in owning the team was to give overlooked athletes with talent an opportunity to step into greater achievement. This was part of the ultimate goal and mission in my heart.

It Was Crazy...

For the next several weeks it was crazy, TV, radio and internet interviews. I knew great things were happening when I was asked to participate in an interview on the Michael Eric Dyson show on Radio One. The Topic was "Female Power Players," in the Sports Industry: on the call was Sheila Johnson, Billionaire Owner of the Washington Team, (WNBA) and Serena Williams. I had to pinch myself, these were women I admired and looked up to in the sports world. During this interview I realized, it wasn't about Alexis Levi, the woman, the daughter, mother and friend. It was about Alexis Levi, making history and opening the doors for men and women around the world to fulfill their dreams as well. I felt compelled to inspire and motivate people to pursue and achieve their goals and destiny in life through my story.

Doors were opening...

I received a call from Karen Waters the daughter of Congresswoman Maxine Waters. She showed so much love and support! She asked, "Is there anything I can do?"

"I'd like to go to the NAACP Image Awards in Los Angeles."

She made a few phone calls and it was done. She called with tickets in her hands and asked me to meet her at the Shrine Auditorium. I was so excited. I sat waiting for the plane and wouldn't you know it, more unplanned surprises. There was an announcement the flight had been cancelled to LA. "Oh, no," I thought and immediately went to the ticket counter. "Ms. we can't get you to Los Angeles until tomorrow," the agent replied smugly to my anxious inquiry. "Are you kidding, I have to be there no later than 6pm after that the doors close to the NAACP awards ceremony. You have to get me to LA," I sounded tormented. "Well, you can fly into Burbank!" the agent responded. "How far is that?" "About an hour from the auditorium," the clerk responded with concern. "There was no way I could miss this event!"

I ended up flying into Burbank and took the one hour cab drive to the Shrine Auditorium for the Image Awards. What a great experience to be sitting in the audience. Owning the Star's was changing my life in so many positive ways. Doors were opening I could never have anticipated in my wildest dreams.

CHAPTER 11
Strive for Success

I wanted to make playing for the Star's a great experience for these basketball players. The athlete's would be treated like professional players. The athletes reported to the gym ready to play. Some players had their game faces on and others walked around as if they were better than their teammates. Each day I received a report from coaches, players and on lookers. The Tark Center was a family environment there were always NBA Players around as well as kids.

One of the players continually challenged the veteran players on and off the court. It was like he was looking for a good fight. Unfortunately, he was one of my best athletes but he had issues mixing with the team on a positive level. One day he spoke too soon and one of the coaches went into a mode where he challenged the "young fella." The coach proceeded to beat this rebellious player down with 'one up shot after the other' that saw the bottom of the net every time!

Soon the whole team stopped playing to witness what was happening. Then voices elevated, curse words transpired, and the arrogant player stormed out of the gym. I received calls from the players and emails from onlookers before the gym was empty. In response I called one of the coaches to inquire about the situation. I wanted to know details, what had happened. He became a little defensive this matter was brought to my attention. "I'm the General Manager, Head of Player Operations, who else do you think they were going to call?"

I realized being a woman in a position of authority was going to be a challenge.

There was an instant entanglement with Matt Winan. One of the coaches felt Matt approached him inappropriately after the incident. It instantly became about Matt instead of disharmony on the team. Suddenly, fingers were pointing, I continued to hear how Matt wasn't right for the team. Rumors began to fly behind my back. Some were accusing, "She must be sleeping with him." I felt so hurt and offended by the crude, abrasive comments. I just believe right is right and wrong is wrong.

The Beast...

A few days later, we lost our Center because of more personality conflicts. He was 6ft 10in, a towering giant with ability. A replacement on short notice wasn't going to be easy to find. There was only two days before our game, what a jam! One of the coaches called a friend of his, Terron Williams, who would meet us for the approaching games. There seemed to be constant bickering, strife and ego conflict. Terron our new center hopped on a plane in LA and met us at the hotel in Phoenix. As the bus pulled up to the hotel I noticed a large man standing in front of the hotel. Terron was 6-6 but he looked more like a football player, a massive wall, very muscular, a true giant. I stepped off the bus surveying his wide structure. Sizing him up I asked, "What do they call you?" "The Beast," he replied with a grin from ear to ear.

The "Woman" Owner...

Our strategy was to win the first two games. We wanted to make a statement about the Las Vegas Stars. Everyone waited to see the team selected to represent the "WOMAN," owner. When we walked in places people took notice. "Who was this woman with the giants?" curious faces inquired with long stares.

I had to chuckle because GT came off the bus dressed in a full suit, for those of you that don't know GT; he's a coach that was not fond of dressing up. He looked great, the LV Stars had arrived. On one occasion I stayed in the bus for a few minutes slightly overjoyed with tears in my eyes. With the help of so many investors and supporters, the season commenced. It was routine to walk off the bus greeted by security, people would stare. I smiled and spoke to all who wanted to say a word. Everyone wanted to get a glimpse of the "First African American Woman to Own a Professional Men's Team."

Stars Douse Flame...

I realized there was no turning back while gazing around the arena. The first game victory was applauding. We won 125-116 the guys were on point, the high scorer for the night was Jason McGowan with 25 points, and second lead was the "Beast" Terron Williams. The headlines read "Stars Douses Flame in Season Opener." We left the arena on a high, slapping five and rejoicing in the first victory. They chanted "Las Vegas Stars! Las Vegas Stars!" as the bus doors closed. The second game was more of the same; this gave the LV Stars respect. We had gone into Phoenix and beat them both games at their home opener. The second game score was 140-105, the Stars used a 47 point third quarter to break open a close game and never looked back. Dejuan Tate led the Stars in double figures with a game high of 28 points. We headed home with a feeling like no other. We were floating, "ON TOP OF THE WORLD!" The bus ride home was a true party, loud Hip Hop music, ESPN Sports on the Flat Screen, with Gatorade flowing!

It was now preparation time for our first home game. We were determined to keep the winning streak alive! We sent press releases out about our first two wins but only got love from a few publications. Finally I received a call from Channel 3, from a reporter who wanted an interview with me and the team. I received a call from Channel 8. We began to do a lot of interviews on TV and the radio. One day channel 8 came to the Stars practice. They took footage of the practice and interviewed me, Sean Higgins, Dejuan Tate and Deavereaux Vinzant: Dajuan for being the high scorer, and Deavereaux for being the youngest player and Sean because he was the assistant coach. GT was not available that day.

Glory hounds...

Our first home game was with the Colorado Crossovers. The score was 151-128. Terron Williams "The Beast" led the Stars in double figures with a game high of 30 points. Dajuan Tate the teams leading scorer added 29 points for a cumulative win.

Whew! We were glory hounds! Life was so sweet. What an unbelievable high. We were on a role but there was drama going on with the coaching staff.

As a team we were in first place and riding high. However, I had to honor the whole team and tried not to get caught in the cross fire which potentially could cause ill feelings thus distracting the focus off winning and on politics.

We won three games in a row but insidiously underlying the initial success was a festering disconnect between me as the General Manager, the coaches and some of the athletes. The second game against the Crossovers, GT sat one of our best players, SH on the bench for the entire first half. These were our first home games and several in the audience had come out to see this athlete. It was not every day they could watch a former NBA Player they were used to seeing only on TV.

At halftime I pulled the coach aside. "Why isn't SH on the floor?" I inquired in a low tone. GT's eyes widened, caught a bit off guard he was being questioned at all. He replied with a short gruff snort, "He told me he didn't want to be on the court." He hurried his words and disappeared into the men's locker room hoping to escape any further questioning.

I proceeded to question SH pulling him aside, "Why are you on the bench?" Sean responded, "I want to play but coach tends to put me in the game when the team gets behind so I can clean up." Without missing a step he kept moving towards the locker room with deflected eyes. I stood perplexed shaking my head. The scenario reminded me of earlier experiences dealing with Dev's coaches. I thought, "Why all the power trips? What are the motives? What was happening to my team?" I was fuming what happened to my team. I couldn't help but feel a stabbing pain surfacing deep within my core. It was hard to ignore the drama being played out in front of me.

CHAPTER 12
Downplay and Deception

My phone kept beeping and buzzing throughout our fourth home game, "Who was calling me repeatedly? Everyone knew I was at our game!" Recognizing the phone number, it was one of my business partners. I answered reluctantly during the game, "Yes, Alexis here." A troubled voice was on the other end, "I'm in financial trouble and there's no way I can continue to invest in the Stars. I have an exorbitant amount of taxes due and the IRS is threatening to lean my assets if I don't make arrangements to pay over the next two months." The call ended as abruptly as it started. I withered in faintness, "How was I going to cover all the costs of running the team as well as provide for my family?" Within moments the Star's financial forecast plummeted. Financially the team was unraveling, receipts for one game depending if we were traveling could run as high as $40,000. I called a meeting after the game and explained to the guys the trouble we were in. We had a few sponsors that owed us money for the season; I would call on them and see if they could expedite their payments. I promised, "I'll do everything in my power to correct this.

Due to the abrupt withdrawal of this main investor by the sixth game of the season we were in a total money crunch. A negative attitude clouded the team and rumors surfaced behind my back. Mysteriously, the players were advised by anonymous voices, "Don't get on the floor unless she pays you." Some of the detracting voices seemed to be there for the glory only and not in it for the long haul. Yet, in the world of sports and business if the finances aren't there then friends run short and relationships are cut quickly. The financial catastrophe naturally put a wedge between me and everyone else. Turmoil increased I realized players and coaches would have to wait to be paid. I found myself crying my eyes out, and headed to the "Boardroom," looking for investors. I was sinking in a pit of bottomless expenses. The economy was in an uproar of depression and a tornado of financial woes invaded the Las Vegas Stars as well.

The coaches ran practice one day and a few of the players didn't show up." This was crazy, how could we be on such a high one week and the next week we were going through drama? Money does the talking in any business.

Forfeit Ownership...

Stress set in, I lost weight and fought depression. I pieced together money to pay the players and the coaches. Word got out, "The Stars were having financial problems." I contacted the Commissioner and was truthful about the situation. "I'll be in Colorado with a team of eight instead of the normal twelve," I broke the news. He agreed but the threat of losing the team was still imminent! I was so stressed it was hard to think. The Colorado games were coming. "How was I going to do this?" I spoke with friends and associates in a desperate plea, trying to figure a way out of the financial devastation.

I was actually trying to pay off as much expense as possible from my own finances. In the midst of phone calling and trying to network it appeared the Star's were losing ground on and off the court. We were still in first place at this time, without a loss. My athletes were valiant, playing and devouring the other teams in the league.

Word was out the Stars were in trouble but what a powerhouse of a team. The unstoppable Star's on the court were hitting a brick wall. It was all crashing in, tempers and arguments flared. "Where was the dream headed?" It felt like sand, sifting through my fingers. Feelings of failure and defeat emerged and saturated my bones with the heaviness of defeat. There was blaming and finger pointing. I was unable to move, the weight of the situation was paralyzing, alarming. My prayer, "Dear

God, where are you now?" I had to keep my faith, realizing God still does miracles today!

Coach Carter

A few weeks passed my grueling schedule and circumstances with the Star's continued. I was working full time as an executive plus managing the Stars. I had multiple personal dilemmas all occurring at the same time. To name a few: Financial issues with the team, my elderly mother, marital separation, raising my sweet understanding Tyler and Deavereaux as well as dealing with the "Boardroom."

I was working the weekend at a conference representing my employer. The inspirational keynote speaker was Coach Carter, basketball coach from Richmond California that had a movie made about his life; A-List Actor Samuel Jackson played his character. Anytime, I could get close to anything related to basketball I was excited. After Coach Carter spoke I thought, "I have to meet him." There were crowds of people surrounding him after he completed his dynamic speech. Everyone wanted to shake his hand. After all he was the man responsible for the story of "Coach Carter." "Well, maybe it just isn't my time to meet this celebrity," I mused.

I had envisioned a movie about the Stars. I wanted everyone to know the ups and downs, the good, bad and ugly. Most of all the persistence it was taking to retain this role of Owner, CEO, and General Manager of the Stars. "Meeting Coach Carter would be so encouraging," I thought. As I walked back to the quiet "Trade Show Room," somewhat disappointed to relieve my co-worker from his duties a sadness flooded my soul. Most attendees were in separate workshops at this time. There were scattered pockets of people walking around the exhibit hall.

All of a sudden I heard voices and looking up to my surprise Coach Carter was coming my way! "Oh my God how do I look? Was my hair and makeup right?" my mind raced in typical female exhilaration. He looked and stopped, "How are you?" For a moment I glanced over my shoulder making sure he wasn't speaking to someone else. His gaze landed on me. I took a big gulp of anxiety and tried to answer in a timely manner. "What's this company about?" he persisted. I began to explain. He said, "You look familiar, I've seen you before!" "Really," I was shocked. He continued, "I've seen your Press Release regarding the Las Vegas Stars." We both became instantly excited and began to talk about my favorite topic, basketball. I commended his accomplishment on the movie. About that time, someone walked up, it was my coworker and Coach Carter bid his farewell. I was so excited. "Wow, Coach Carter knows who I am!"

No one at my job realized I was the new found owner of the Las Vegas Stars. I wanted to ease into this new title realizing it may cause a problem with my employer. The day went on and as the exhibit room was winding down for a planned reception. I saw what looked like Coach Carter coming towards me again. He said, "Hey, I wanted to ask you one more thing about your team." This time my coworker was there and he was all ears. I tried to steer Coach Carter away but it was too late, my co worker began to ask questions too.

No turning back...

Later that evening I placed a call to my office to speak to my boss regarding some business. Alarmed, I detected a change in the tone of her voice, "I want to see you first thing in the morning." I wondered if the news about the Stars had reached her ears, by a so called "coworker." My gut instinct detected trouble ahead. The new disclosure could place my position in jeopardy because most corporations require their employee's body, soul and spirit. Ownership if you know what I mean. They expect your life to be completely devoted and dedicated to the company, working ten to twelve hour days without questions.

I flew home early the next morning from the conference to do an interview with Barbara Rodgers, KPIX Ch 5. I was still feeling uneasy about my manager's tone. Suppressing the nagging thoughts, I pushed forward, the interview went well. Then I left the set of KPIX and headed to work with a pit of anxiety in my stomach.

It was as if I had a premonition the 'ax' was ready to fall in the "Boardroom." How often I had seen it before, a devoted employee's desk cleared and possessions neatly packed into corporate boxes, waiting for them when they entered the office in the morning. It's amazing how close business friendships can be cut and ousted so quickly if your commitment seems compromised. I reached for the corporate office door and paused to take a deep breath. The boss wants to see me, we all know what that means most of the time. I realized in my heart of hearts it wasn't for pats on the back and a hand shake of congratulations. I needed the income from this position and was desperate without it.

I was pouring money into the Stars along with the other investors, the costs were enormous. It was at this moment I knew there was no turning back, there would be sacrifices along the way, plenty of them. And this would prove to be one of many.

As I entered the office her back was to me, apparently admiring the view outside the window. She swirled the chair around. "Have a seat," she motioned with a cutting hand and a cold, calculating voice. I felt like a naughty kid sent to the Principals office or a dishonest employee who was caught stealing. The spirit of corporate betrayal was in the air. I was the guilty, she was the offended.

According to my performance record, I felt my job wasn't suffering. I wasn't going to neglect my position, if anything I was working harder. Honestly, I felt my obligations as a corporate employee were being fulfilled. I just came back from working all weekend for this company, and reported to work bright and early Monday morning. I was giving far more of my life to the company than was reciprocated.

A punch of anxiety hit my stomach and evolved into a ball of nerves. She lowered her bifocals to rest on the tip of her nose and gazed at some papers in her hands. She cleared her throat and began in with a whine, "First of all I was quite shocked to hear of your new found business venture with the Las Vegas Stars. You hadn't mentioned a thing to me or the corporate office about your side business." Her eyes flirted with condescension in a punishing fashion. I definitely offended the powers of corporate the only thing left to do was to sit and take the beating. She continued with a twinge of anger, "As you know we expect dedication from our staff, this position is taxing and requires full time, plus devotion." She took a deep breath and then went in for the kill, "We, the corporate office congratulate you for your new found success. On the other hand, you have been terminated from your position, due to your extracurricular commitments and obligations outside this office." It appeared she took pleasure in bearing the crushing news. I knew it was pointless to argue the point. "Prove any job negligence?" I wanted to argue the point. I had seen it all too often in the boardroom, the slicing and dicing of positions. Some for legitimate reasons others just to serve the company's expectations. Once corporate decisions were made it was like fighting city hall to reverse the verdict. Refusing to allow further humiliation I collected my things and walked out the door and into a new destiny. "The LOCKER ROOM was again... calling."

At that moment I heard vast numbers of people from all around the world cheering me on. I received emails from supporters asking for advice or relating how my story encouraged them to move forward with their own unfulfilled dreams. I was paying a price for owning the Stars. This was just the beginning of many grueling tests, agonizing situations and rejections along the way. A price had to be paid. The financial demands never stopped rolling in, rent, car payment, groceries and the team. "Dear God, I'm famous and in the financial struggle of my life. I'm in trouble!" In summation I was fired; losing a $100,000 + dollar a year job. My hefty savings and personal investments were plummeting. Talk about devastation, I was living it, one disaster after the other.

The dilemma surrounding the Colorado games was still an issue and rapidly approaching. I was not only devoid of additional investors but I was also unemployed. Soon afterwards, I began receiving calls from sleazy predators stating they wanted to invest in the Stars. Realizing their ultimate goals, I heard through rumor, their ulterior motives were to tear the team from my grasp. Everyone seemed to turn on me, all but some of the players. Other players began leading a negative bandwagon of complaints.

The league official hung up the phone rather disappointed we were muscling through despite the challenges. It's amazing how some people have no problem kicking you when you're down.

We made it to Colorado the Stars fought their way through and lost the two games, 165-117 and 158-138. Not too shabby as the league insisted we add unknown Colorado players to our roster to complete the team. We lost and it was no surprise, we weren't even the Stars but a makeshift team hoping for the best! Our spirits were broken yet we still continued to pursue our goal of becoming champions.

Life was crazy but I was determined to get through it! I was talking to a friend of mine and she encouraged me to speak to two investment associates of hers. One of them was especially interested in the LV Stars, he saw the vision. He wanted to take it to his capital group. I was excited; maybe this was a way out of this tornado. They came back to me a few days later and stated, "The partners did not want to make a large investment at this time." But I was grateful for a small investment they provided inch by inch, step by step the foundation was being built.

It was a roller coaster flying from the tracks. I remember driving and pulling over to the side of the road and breaking down in tears more than once. I asked, "God help me through this." It wasn't about the money; it was about not letting my team down. They had worked hard and they deserved to finish the season on top.

One day I was sitting at home with tears in my eyes wondering how I was going to get through this. I received a conference call from Dajuan Tate, Eddie Shelby and Willie Hall: During the conversation they reaffirmed their commitment to the Stars and supported me as their General Manager. Their affirming voices meant the world to me at such a low point. "Alexis, we need to put Colorado behind us and get back in the business of winning games." Their confidence bolstered me and I said, "Let's fight for this."

Willie Hall, a teacher at one of the Las Vegas High Schools, offered the gym for a few practices. Dajuan Tate recommended a friend who would eventually see the Star's through as coach to complete the season. He was employed by a local supplement company and wanted to work with the Las Vegas Stars as a joint promotion. The company would allow him to coach the Star's and use their company motor coach for travel.

I lost a few players after they were given their last checks, Jason McGowan, Deandre Hewitt and Terron Williams the "Beast," left. I don't blame them and was very sorry to see them go. The Star's remaining players began to look for replacement athletes to fill the roster. Dajuan called a friend, Waki Williams who had just returned from playing overseas.

GT and SH also had enough with the Star's money woes which was completely understandable. I don't blame them and was very thankful for their hard work and dedication to the Star's for part of our first season. Despite all the chaos, drama, and movement of players and coaches, the Stars were back at it.

Yes, with a few new players and a new coach we were even more determined than ever. The human spirit at its best was seen in these remarkable, dedicated players and coaches. In their honor I want to list the names of those who stayed till the end of the season and were rewarded with playoff publicity and All Star Games, way to go, guys. Hats off to: Deaveraux Vinzant, Eddie Shelby, Hollis Hale, Willie Hall, Matt Winans, Dajuan Tate, Trevor Lawrence, Waki Williams, Demetrius Orme, Herve Gibson, Jonathan Walker, and Maurice Thomas. This group of valiant men believed in the impossible. These athletes also looked beyond themselves and thought about others.

Shortly after the Colorado games we were contacted by a former NBA Player who was directing an athletic program at Western High School. We would pay the High School and use their gym as a way for them to raise funds for their underserved athletic program. Now, this was one of the reasons I was motivated to see this season through. It's one of my visions to see unfortunate youth have the opportunities to experience basketball clinics with professional basketball athletes in Las Vegas and around the country.

The saga continued, on June 8-9, 2007, we were to play Santa Barbara. I heard from the Commissioner they were adding all kinds of power players just to come in and beat the Stars. Unbeknownst to them the Stars original team was splintered and it would take a few games to reach a competitive level. We were a team basically learning how to work together, it wasn't a surprise the upset was painful. The headlines read, "The Breakers Top the Stars with Hot Shooting," final score 155-127. The Breakers were deadly from the perimeter in the victory shooting, 23 of 46 from the three point range, ouch. Fred Vinson on the Breakers hit 9 of 14 three pointers to finish with a team high of 35. Dajuan Tate of the LV Stars fought back with a 40 point high, but it just wasn't enough. The LV Stars tried but they had lost their momentum.

The next day I arrived early before the second game against the Breakers. I called the team together for a pep talk. "Is this team that much better than you guys, no?" my voice sounded insistent and matter of fact. I continued, "Did they play smarter than you guys last night? They have three good shooters that made all their points. All you have to do is shut them down and you'll limit their scoring." The second game against the Breakers wasn't going well. The half time break came with a sigh of relief and frustration for most of the Stars. I was sitting on the sidelines next to Deaveraux who was fuming with disappointment. I turned to Dev and said, "You need to tell them to shut down, Toby Bailey, and run them so they get tired." I had a young team and they definitely had more energy than the seasoned Breakers team.

Dev looked at me and hastily raised his voice. "You go tell them." Rather embarrassed I blasted, "They're in the locker room!" He said to me, "Mom, you're the boss you can go anywhere, including the locker room." I stood up straightened my jacket while gazing into my son's flustered expression. I needed that extra push, our eyes locked he nodded his head towards the locker room.

Looking back I had to be both strong and harsh as a father and nurturing and doting as any mother. At that moment I was looking into the eyes of a man, who was no longer my little son. "Go get em Bootsy, you're a fighter," he teased with his deep voice and a big smile. It was basically the first time I had entered the "Locker Room." In the distance I could hear the coach firing corrections in frustration.

The team was wringing wet drenched in perspiration with towels draped around their necks. They were hanging on every word while wiping their brows. I walked around a wall of lockers then all eyes shifted in my direction. The coach stopped his train of thought in respect for my entrance. He nodded his head and gave me the floor. "Listen guys, this seasoned Breaker team is mature so the strategy is to out run them. You guys are young and fast, wear them down. Also, shut down their big shooters, double team them, do what it takes, but don't let them make those shots."

The players nodded with respect, the coach looked at me as if to verify I was done. I nodded and then walked out of the locker room. Before the half they were outscored 37-16. In the second half the Stars rallied to take a 113-110 lead in the final period before the Breakers took control for good. The Breakers player, Trayvon Lathan had his second consecutive triple-double with a game high of 31 points, 16 rebounds and 10 assists. Toby Bailey recorded a double in the win, finishing with 30 points and 10 rebounds, all for a Breakers win. Eddie Shelby led the LV Stars with 29 points in the loss. As we came together to discuss the game I encouraged the team, "The Breakers first 5 were former NBA players. You guys played an NBA game tonight and have nothing to be ashamed about." We prepared to leave the gym. We may have lost but the competition was considered as the Stars gave there all.

The next day I attended the SPA Odyssey Event as one of the panelists. The event was to include some of the most prestigious minority women in the world. I complained to my friend Mary, "I don't feel prestigious at this moment." She blasted, "Do you think these women achieved their positions without going through trials, heart break and troubles? It's about what you're accomplishing, the doors that you're opening. You need to go and enjoy the legacy your building." I decided despite all the negative circumstance in my life I would forge ahead and take this opportunity to meet people. It proved to be a wonderful event, I was treated like a queen. I wondered, "What if I had allowed frustrations and my downcast spirit to prevent my attendance at this function?"

So, often in life we miss out on many great experiences because we allow our emotions to dictate our comings and goings. Through this whole journey I've found good friends and a wise word spoken in season to be indispensable. At the event I first met Kim Dubard and then the executive of the organization. I began to connect with powerful women from all over the world who were inspired by my success and my knowledge. I provided insights into the business of franchising. It was after taking that step of faith I realized in life when everything looks its worst, God is still in control and moving us closer to our destiny, despite all the issues, problems, crisis and turmoil. In May of 2007, I was also asked to be on a business panel for the '100 Black men Event' in Las Vegas. I met successful business people from the African American business world and this proved interesting and an opportunity for more networking.

CHAPTER 13
Winners Circle

I received a call from the owner of the Phoenix Flame's they were also experiencing financial difficulties. A Sponsorship had fallen through and caused a hardship for the team. They were told to call and ask permission to reschedule the games. It's interesting because the owner of this team wasn't threatened in regards to losing ownership of the team by the league. I was asked, "Can you change the date of the game to accommodate our financial issues?" At first I thought, "Okay." But after speaking to my players, they reminded me of the pressures and threats bestowed upon the Stars financial woes. "What about all the cast iron league rules?" they questioned. Then I called the Commissioner and asked some pointed questions, "It's obvious there's a different standard of rules and options depending on what team you're dealing with?" I left him with that thought and requested the two games be forfeited. At the end of the day, they were. Generally I'm more forgiving but at this point my nerves were frayed so thin it was difficult to find compassion.

Meanwhile, my resume' was impressive and impeccable but for the first time in my life I couldn't find a job. The world was going through a major financial tailspin. Like the rest of my life, I knew there had to be a reason for all of this. I began to watch the news and people who had stable lives were losing their homes and financial security. Investments I had committed to were going south. Major corporations were withdrawing their sponsorship commitments and some were even going out of business. Multi-Million dollar companies that had been around for years were shutting their doors. After prayer I decided to walk through the doors that were open and to not look back.

The economy was declining into recession, real estate prices were plummeting, and unemployment was rising. It was early spring 2007, we were headed for the playoffs yet I had no idea how God was going to pull this off. I was doing everything in my power, from networking to soliciting supporters and investors. The debt collectors were calling, everyone had their hand out. It seemed life was throwing every curve, twist and hard ball imaginable. I was living a complete faith walk and so far out of my comfort zone there was no turning back. Any sense of pride was dashed, this experience was completely humbling. I was working harder then ever maintaining the team with constant phone calls trying to solicit supporters.

There were times when I felt numb and had to pinch myself, was all this really happening? Thank God my sons were healthy and pulling with me every step of the way. My son's Deavereaux and Tyler were my greatest supporters. One night a soft voice echoed in my ears, "Mom." Tyler reached to put his long arm around my shoulder. He felt the pain and frustration I was trying so hard to hide, "Keep going, you can't give up now." Tears began to roll down my cheeks uncontrollably, "What was I doing dragging Tyler through all this?" I thanked God for Tyler's friends and their families that rallied behind me and literally helped care for him for several months during this whole process.

The season pressed on the new coach prepared for the next two game series in Arizona. Matt Winans, a native from Arizona arranged for the team to stay at a three bedroom exclusive membership condominium in Scottsdale Arizona. It was a great trip; everyone seemed to get along great. We were a team again and we came to Arizona to retrieve our winning streak. Some guys slept on the coaches, the beds, and the floors, the place was wall to wall giants. I ordered ten pizzas that night and they had a good time talking up the next few games.

We played the two games and won, the Stars were on the move. One of the games the score was 181/142, this game was special because my son Deavereaux Vinzant was on the list of the high scorers with 24 points. We headed back on the road to Las Vegas as victors. The new players, Waki Williams, Elliot Orme and Trevor Lawrence were great. As we headed home, I began to plan for an eight game run at home. As I stated earlier, the cost of running a team is rather expensive. I had eight home games in a row. I had pulled some money to pay for part of the bills but how was I going to make it through this pricey challenge. I was encouraged to have a conference call with 30 of my closest friends and associates. Business Associates encouraged me, "You don't need to do this by yourself, you need a team of people to support you." That night, we had a conference call with over 40 people. We discussed the immediate needs for the team and asked for assistance. The next day, I called my oldest friend in the world, Karyn. I asked her to be on the call solely for the purpose of making sure God was on this call. I needed her prayers desperately.

Triumph...

I felt the triumphs and struggles in owning the Star's. I was going through an enormous battle of my life not only with the Star's but it seemed I was wrestling with a greater power. God was using these struggles to remold me into a vessel to be used for His glory. He in many ways was humbling and reworking my heart in the areas of family, finances, purpose and security I had grown accustomed to over years were gone. In adult life my history was one of prosperity, stability, and success but now I found myself on shaky ground. I knew something had to happen in order to complete the 2007 season. The door suddenly opened.

The next day I called Karyn asking for prayer. "Karyn, I've been praying I don't know what else to do," my voice withered in despair. She said, "Alexis, I want to invest in the Las Vegas Stars." There was a moment of silence, unbelievable, I was speechless. I broke the silence, "Do you mean it?" I responded, "You aren't going to believe this but I feel so strongly that God wants me to help get the Star's through the season and to the playoffs." "I've been pleading with God to get the Star's through this season. He's answering my prayers," I gasped in amazement.

There are times in our lives when the Lord chooses servants to assist people in reaching their destiny. There has been several times during this journey where God has brought key people forward to complete the purchase of the team, assist with the season, help provide for our needs, and helped acquire scholarships for college and more. I find that as long as I patiently wait, the Lord sees me through. We are all here for a special purpose to come into relationship with him and help those around us. As God answered my prayers for help, I went to work to see the Star's through their first season. A difficult time, now became a great time for the Las Vegas Star's to shine. By the end of the season many of the players were able to go to the next level.

Back to the drawing board...

The Las Vegas Stars were back in business and it was back to the drawing board. We had a game scheduled whereby we were to play an All Star team in an exhibition game. The Stars scored 200 points that night, we were so excited. We called the league and the Commissioner told me, "It's not necessary to publicize the win because it wasn't an official league game." The win was spectacular because no team in the league had ever done this and it was really unbelievable! The Star's were disappointed because we needed the positive press and exposure for the athletes who were trying to excel to the next level of basketball and finance. The news leaked out to the press and the next day I received a few calls.

Playing for the kids...

As we prepared for our last two games, we connected with a nearby community center where 3000 children attended for summer programs. We went to the center to ask if the kids would like the Star's to play two games at the center. After all the ups and downs, we decided to play for the kids and donate the last two games of the season. The stands were full of kids that would not be able to afford to see our games. The Stars shined, we played the Phoenix Flames for a game win of 153/136. Then the next day the Star's won 206/128, it was a legitimate league game. The Stars were determined that the league was going to give us credit for blowing the competition away with another 200 point game.

The Stars set a league record; this was the first time, but really the second in league history that a team scored 200 points in a league game. God still does miracles today!

After the game, the kids were so excited, running around getting autographs from their favorite Star player. I was so proud of the Star's these men really cared about making the kids happy and took the time to shake hands, sign autographs, and talk with the children. The children's faces gleamed with excitement the Star's had made their day. What special people God had brought my way. Each player from the Las Vegas Stars came over and shook the hands of the Coach and the General Manager, little ole me. "Well we made it," they exclaimed! "What a great season," others added. Euphoria was in the air, my mind and focus was headed to the playoffs.

Showoff at the playoffs...

In a week the Stars would go to the playoffs and face the top teams in the West. Karyn booked a flight and met us in Portland, "I'm going to see you through Alexis and the Stars will do great!" she was my best cheerleader. The weather was partly cloudy but what a beautiful city Portland, Oregon is for so many to enjoy. The Star's arrived and began to prepare.

It was the 'playoff' games! As I sat and looked around at the teams, the stands, the crowd in a buzz, the referees preparing to begin the game, I realized this was it. What we had been waiting for, to go to the playoffs as a first year professional men's basketball team was an accomplishment all of its own. The Las Vegas Stars had made it.

As the referee's whistle blew and the time clock sounded to signal the players it was time to go to the bench and prepare for what would be the first of many appearances at the playoffs for the Las Vegas Stars, I was astounded by the moment.

The lights gleamed from the score board, the sports castors readied to announce the opponents. The national anthem was being sung and each player stood motionless in respect and complete attention to salute the American Flag. Moments later our coach called the first five players to take the floor, Karyn looked over at me with a great big smile we were ready for more battles. I looked up to heaven and said, "Thank you Dad and God."

The Stars were matched with the Portland Chinooks, the 2006 Champions. The Star's battled through a tightly contested first half before Portland took over the second half. Many of the officials were looking nervous, "Was it possible for the Star's to beat the Chinooks?" The first half was so tight within two points the whole time. Regretfully, the Stars lost to the champions. Though the Stars lost in the playoffs, they felt really good about what the team achieved in the season. The playoff weekend proved a success when four of the Stars were chosen for the 'All Star' game the following day. The athlete's selected from the Star's were Dajuan Tate, Willie Hall, Eddie Shelby, and Hollis Hale.

Following the season I was honored in August, 2007 with the Egretha Award for the achievement of being the first African American Woman to own a Men's Professional Basketball team which also served the underserved youth of Las Vegas. This award was given at the WBBC's annual Women's Business Conference in Chicago.

Then in October, 2007 I was asked to be one of the chairwomen for the National Association of Black Female Entertainment Media Executives Conference. Some of the other chairwomen were Mona Scott CEO and Lisa Ellis CEO for Sony Company. The opportunity and experience was memorable and I continued to network for the Star's next season.

CHAPTER 14
Season II

The Las Vegas Community was happy to see us return bigger, better and stronger.

The newspapers were calling for interviews, radio stations wanted to cover the games and I got a call from the MGM Corporate Diversity Department to be the Keynote Speaker for the Women of Color Conference. As we prepared for the season, we realized that all of our players were returning for the second season except Deavereaux Vinzant, who returned to school and Dajuan Tate, who signed a contract with the Chinese Basketball Association.

As the Commissioner began to plan the season schedule, I requested that the Star's athletes be allowed to travel on the West and East Coast. This would give the players more visibility. It was my goal to have the players leave the Stars after a year or two and go overseas or on to the NBA. Traveling with the team to Los Angeles, Phoenix, Colorado, Detroit and Chicago was great. One day we were at an airport and several travelers inquired as to whom these tall men where, the tallest player on the Stars was Trevor Lawrence. He was 7 ft. tall and our Center. All of the Las Vegas Star's athletes stood from 6 ft. 3 to 7 ft tall. So when we were all together, we appeared as a force to be reckoned with. The kids would often come up and ask for autographs when they would see us walking down the corridor.

The stewardesses went crazy as well, often getting in trouble for flirting with the players. I don't know what it is but there is something about athletes that excites people. We'd rent vans when visiting an area and I often enjoyed our evenings out on the town. Every night we would all go out to have a team dinner. I'd often have to scope out a restaurant that served food in large quantities like buffets, boy could those big guys eat! It was like going out with a family of twelve giants. Sometimes the waitresses would get harassed and other times the waitresses would give the guys a hard time but it was all done in "fun."

As we headed for games some of the athletes bobbed their heads listening to music through headphones, others wore sunglasses and sat in complete silence, a few chatted with teammates about the plan to devour the opponent.

After arriving to game venues onlookers stood by eyeballing the Las Vegas Stars and the General Manager. It was like I was a "freak of nature" instead of a woman who loved sports.

Opportunities exploded, I was chosen to represent Pepsi in a National Calendar, entitled "Family First." I accepted the offer to be a part of this historical publication. I always wanted to be a model but never had the discipline to lose another 10 pounds. I had the opportunity to travel first class to New York City and stayed in a beautiful hotel suite with enough room for ten people. Then I traveled by limousine and did a photo shoot like a Top Model. "Wow, I couldn't believe this was really happening!"

You never know where God is going to place you. After the shoot, I met the National Pepsi representative we looked over the photos of the day she chose the one she liked the best. I returned to the hotel enjoying a great sleep. I arose early the next morning to a tremendous breakfast and a note that read, "A car would be waiting in front of the hotel to take me to the airport at 11am." As we weaved the streets of New York the driver took me on a sightseeing tour of the city. Everyone was very nice, I was grateful for the opportunity to do what others only dream of in their lives. I was still waiting for someone to "pinch me" and wake me up from this fantastic dream.

One day I received a text saying "I loved your picture in Ebony." I ignored it thinking it had to be a mistake. I soon received another, "I loved your picture in Essence." I started to get a little curious so I called one of my friends back and they assured me it was me on a Pepsi advertisement. This was crazy, I figured it was for the calendar but I had no idea what had just happened. I became curious so I went out to grab a bite of food and I found myself in the magazine isle of Walgreens. I picked up the Ebony Magazine and as I fingered through the pages I landed on the one with me, there I was holding two basketballs. "Wow, is that me?" It's amazing what a great makeup artist and hair stylist can do. I wanted to scream but laughed instead hysterically, so much so that tears began to stream down my cheeks.

I slowly walked to the counter pulled out my wallet and paid for the magazine. The checker eyed me real strange a witness to my outburst of hysterics. Something prompted me to go back and look in ten other magazines and there I was in all of them. I asked the cashier as I was heading out when the calendar would be available and she assured me it would come out the first of February. The calendar was to be given to all customers at Walgreens and CVS, this was great! What a blessing!

After this occurred I'd go to our games, the woman, children and even men would come up and congratulate me and sometimes ask for an autograph. The opportunities began to roll in 'Indigo Magazine' had done a cover story in January that would come out in the February Issue. Funny thing, they sent me the January issue and Senator Barack Obama was on the cover, I thought to myself what is going on, this is incredible.

I began receiving offers to write a book, opportunities for television and the offer to do a film about my life. I was so grateful for all these things that one day I was driving in my car and stopped at a stop light. I was overjoyed with tears so much so that the cars behind me began honking for me to move on. I had found my purpose.

One day I received an email from a lady that lived in Chicago. She told me she'd seen me in Indigo Magazine. She stated, "My daughter wants to do her Black History Report on you." I was flattered. Something whispered in my ear, "Call her that will make her day." I've always been very down to earth even with all the accolades. I was just a person who was living out her dream.

So I pulled out my cell, dialed her number and she answered. For a moment there was silence on the phone. I realized how much this meant to this family. She talked for a while and then called the young girl to the phone. She was so excited, "Can I schedule you to do an interview?" Of course I stated, "Yes." Out of all the compliments I received this meant the most because it was one of the ways of giving back and remembering where we all come from. So many people become successful and achieve notoriety and fame and they forget they were once a "fan," or the child that looked up to someone. Sudden exposure began to trickle over to the team and then the League. This was exactly what my plan was from the beginning. Little did I know, most of the other team owners were supportive, only a few didn't like, "The first woman." The Stars began to gain momentum other investors surfaced and opportunities were coming in daily. This had grown into the opportunity of a lifetime.

I was speaking with a good friend Sylvester Franklin who was a long-time supporter of the Las Vegas Stars. He introduced me to Laura Herlovich of PR Plus. Her team went to work opening doors and more exposure opportunities in Las Vegas. "Vegas," is a funny town, with all the entertainment available it's better to align with companies that have been a part of Vegas for a long time. The Stars aligned with Children's Organizations, and Senior Programs that allowed a few of the seniors to play in a basketball game with several LV Stars.

We were asked to join the LV Sports Magazine in a community event. The LV News Media supported our efforts and began writing some really good articles. The Review Journal, the LV Weekly, LV Luxury Magazine and more. Skepticism was at an all-time high the first year but tensions eased the second year. That is why I fought so hard to keep the LV Stars going. The fight was on to get the Stars to the playoffs again. Despite, all the publicity and fame this wasn't going to get us the wins on the court. The team was determined to win the title of "Southwest Champions." It was my job to keep them structured and calm so that the team could focus on their destiny.

The Las Vegas community supported us for the most part. However, I can remember times when there were great audiences and other times if an NBA game was on TV, there would be little support. Funny thing I began to be a centerpiece for those involved in the D League, NBA and Overseas Teams. I had to ask myself, "What's going on?" Athletes and coaches from around the world wanted to play or coach for the Las Vegas Stars. I wasn't sure what turns my life was going to take in the months to come. I was torn between my dream and my responsibilities at home. Even though my sons wanted me to go for this dream to build a legacy, it took a heavy toll on the family.

There were times when I wanted to be at home with my son and I was on the road making a way for someone else's son. Often I'd call my sons after a five day road trip and just wanted to cry because I missed them. But they said, "If you want to be in a man's world you have to be tough and do what a man often does." But I was single and relied on friends and family to assist me in keeping life balanced. I remember the day I was sitting with Tyler's godfather and he said, "There's going to come a day when you won't be able to be here for Tyler games." I swore up and down that would never happen. I candidly said, "I make the schedule." Well lo and behold, that day came.

One night we were traveling home and I missed the last flight to the San Francisco Bay Area. Tyler, a sophomore, was receiving an award the next day for 'Most Valuable Player' on the Varsity High School Basketball Team. As tired as I was I took my bag through it in my trunk and proceeded to California at 12 midnight. The drive to Northern California is 8 - 9 hours depending on your speed. I made it there in eight hours. Unfortunately, I didn't account for the peak hour traffic, by the time I navigated through the traffic side streets I missed my baby boy's trophy ceremony. I remember feeling like someone socked me in my stomach. I was the type of mother that was at every game, every award ceremony and most tournaments. "This wasn't fair! How could I balance where I was supposed to be with where I wanted to be?" I questioned. It was so hard to turn away from your own to go and assist another parent's child. I picked Tyler up he was forgiving. We had the best time celebrating with dinner and a movie. He looked at me knowing I had driven over 8 hours and said, "Mom you're the best mom ever. I love you."

There's a price to be paid for success. Even though I thought I was doing a hell of a balancing act, the pyramid was destined to shift. I started seeing cracks in the foundation of good intentions. My older son Dev seemed a bit unbalanced, having to deal with things in life he hadn't experienced before such as career decisions, basketball decisions and life decisions. My younger son was growing up. He was an excellent student but was discovering girls, and going to proms. He was "feeling himself," as the elders used to say because he was a Star Athlete.

One day Tyler decided he'd restructure the original set up of staying with Ms. Dee a trusted, longtime friend. Instead he decided to stay at a teammate's house. This had everyone in an uproar. Other parents began to gossip about my parenting skills and supposed negligence. "How can she go off and develop her dream when her son is moving from house to house?" Oh! I was furious. I was attempting to build a foundation and a legacy for my family and in no way wanted to abdicate my responsibility as a parent. It seemed none of them were willing to go above and beyond the call of duty. They didn't understand that this was not something I necessarily wanted to do , I had to do it. To be honest, if I had to do it over again, I'm not sure I'd agree. The journey can be so painful. The cost was so high. Anyone who knows me realized, "I LOVE," my boys and would never do anything to harm or hurt them in any way. All my efforts were sacrificial I suffered great personal loss and humiliation at times to hopefully build a legacy for my children and grandchildren.

I was on the road with the Stars. We just arrived in Arizona preparing for more games. I was sitting in a meeting with the coaches when my cell phone went off. "Alexis, this is Auntie. You need to get home your mom is critically ill and needs to go to the hospital." She stated, "You need to call 911." "How was I to call California 911 from Arizona?" I agonized. I called the operator in Scottsdale and she connected me to the operator in California and they called 911. Then I contacted the place where Mom lived and let them know the situation and that I was on my way. I caught a redeye flight to California in the wee hours of the morning following our games.

The stress of being an only child, single parent and General Manager of the Las Vegas Stars was overwhelming at times. In a positive light the Stars went on to win the games in Arizona. In the midst of it all I continued to speak around the US receiving awards such as, "Essence

Top 50 Influential Women" and "Ebony Top 150 Most Influential African Americans."

Woman's world...

The LV Stars went on to win Southwest Championship for the IBL, despite all the trials and tribulations encountered. Once the season was over another life check was in order. This venture sent my family into a tail spin. "Should I continue the dream if it meant leaving my family members in compromising circumstances?" I stayed up many nights praying to God for the answer. "It's sometimes easier to make these difficult decisions in a Man's World." But I lived in a "Woman's World," where I felt the brunt of caring for my family on several major levels. I was also influencing major sectors of society, such as the children in the Las Vegas community, the families of the team, the African American community and The Women in Business Community.

The weight of the world was on my shoulders and only God had the blue prints to the plan. I was at the hospital with my mother again and I was dealing with the State authorities. A woman from the Senior Center who befriended my mother placed her name on my mother's bank account. If this wasn't enough the franchise fees for the league were due immediately. I called upon one of my sponsors and he attempted to assist me by going to the bank on the deadline date to pay the franchise fee. "Whew!" I said that was a close one without the fee being paid on time the Stars would be dropped from the league. I will never forget, it was a Friday, the Sponsor stated he was forwarding money into this account and it would be there. On Monday afternoon the Commissioner called, "The check for your franchise fee has bounced. You missed the deadline to play in the league. Sorry I'll have to pull the team." I was so angry due to the fact I had brought so much publicity to the IBL. "Give me a chance to clear this up. Can I please have an extension?"

I found out later others had their eyes on the Las Vegas Market for basketball and basically wanted the Las Vegas Stars to drift into oblivion. I prayed about it and surrendered the dream for a season. I needed to see my son through High School and my mother needed a more stable environment. My dream had to be placed on hold but we all know, "The earth is the Lord's and the fullness thereof." God owns everything and he was in control of the Las Vegas Stars future. He's Lord over every season, just when you think we've lost, we find he never stops working behind the scenes.

I sat back and watched the IBL begin their next season 2009. This would have been the third season for the LV Stars. I realize that increase comes from above. I didn't seek to be the Frist African American Woman to own a Men's Basketball Team and be the GM/CEO. The dream was to build a team and legacy for my boys. God did the rest it was his divine plan that set this all in place. A peace filled my heart about surrendering the team. One night I sat at the dinner table and looked across and saw my beautiful family. A still small voice spoke, "There'll be plenty of time for this later, don't worry."

The Speaking Engagements continued to roll in. In the upcoming months, I continued to work with athletes as a sports and branding agent. Often I consulted other team owners, athletes, and sports programs for free.

My mother began to have increased health issues which needed my undivided attention. In 2010, Tyler graduated from high school. I was able to be at all his high school basketball games and every award and accolade ceremony. He received the MVP award for Desert Pines High School. I saw him off to his Senior Prom he had grown into a young man. After much prayer and hectic last minute decisions and breakthroughs Tyler headed to college on a full ride scholarship. This was God's doing.

In 2011, my life was not my own, I traveled back and forth from Las Vegas to California sometimes two to three times a month to take care of my mom. It was becoming evident time was growing closer for her to cross over the other side to be with the Lord and my Dad. In May 2011, Tyler was home from college, we decided to get the family (My Sons) and my boyfriend together. We traveled to Atlanta, Georgia for a week, "What a great time we had." It was a time of healing and a much needed break for all of us. This was the first time we were able to take a vacation in a few years. I was exhausted and needed refreshment. It was so much fun to see my "two little boys," now grown young men. "God fulfilled my death bed requests from years before," I thought staring into their mature eyes. We ate, slept, shopped and played. Deavereaux proceeded to show Tyler his apartment and music and video production studio. It was a gift to see them get along like they were best friends.

In January 2012, I received a call from the hospital in California. "Your mother is critically ill," the nursing supervisor reported. It was news no one wants to hear about a loved one, especially a parent. It was only my Mom and I since I was 10 years old. I spoke with my boyfriend, Greg and began to cry, "What should I do?" The only choice was to leave Las Vegas and return to California. I called my aunt and she encouraged, "Come and stay your mother needs you." Mom had stopped eating, didn't talk much at the time and she appeared ready to check out on life. She was eighty eight years old. I committed to feeding her three meals a day. It was touch and go for a minute. Suddenly she began to smile more and then her appetite increased. One step at a time, she began to look a lot better. One night Greg and I were at the Hospital, she was smiling, tapping her toes and listening to Gospel Music. Her face lit up like a Christmas tree when we played her favorite song "Leaning on Jesus." After a few songs, she began to yawn so Greg and I prepared her for bed and then left. We were pretty exhausted as well. We had been going to the hospital twice a day for weeks. It actually looked like we were going to pull through this one.

Early the next morning at 1:30am my cell phone rang. It was the hospital beckoning me to come immediately. Mom was in respiratory distress and they had been working on increasing her oxygen levels up for about an hour. The doctor asked, "Do you still want us to intubate her?" That was her request but no chest compressions. I hopped out of bed with the room swirling around me and woke up everyone in the house. My first thought was to rush but then I was reminded that the Man upstairs was in control. No amount of rushing was going to keep my mother if the Lord was ready to take her home. I stopped and prayed. After prayer we headed to the hospital. Greg and I walked into ICU to see her frail frame gasping for breath. She laid there suffering with her eyes open. The doctors gave us the solemn truth, "It was only a matter of time."

My belief in God and my own personal healing helped us retain faith for the impossible. Even when I was with the Las Vegas Stars I'd never let them give up until the game was over. Talking to the doctors was similar to a locker room pep talk. I asked Greg, "What do we do when things look impossible? But you know there's a chance for a final 3 points at the buzzer, you believe, you believe you believe!"

We decided to continue the journey. Mom gestured to the Nurse Practitioner, "She wanted to live." She lived for a while with the help of a ventilator and a feeding tube. When she was discharged to Alameda Health Center, the nurses and doctors complemented our faith. They said, "Because of your faith your mother is living longer. She's doing better." Miracles still happen today!

Mom lived three months longer than anyone would have believed. One night her eyes spoke volumes, "I'm ready to go." That night I kissed her forehead so many times I think she was annoyed. The doctor stopped by, "There's nothing else we can do." A few days earlier I asked her, "Are you going to stay with me a few more years?" She shook her head slightly in the gesture to say "I don't know." I asked again the day before she passed, "Are you going to stay with me?" The response changed to "No." The night before she passed she stared at me unable to speak but her teary eyes spoke volumes. Greg played a song from You Tube, "He has you in his hands," by Marvin Sapp. She closed her eyes and began making her ascent. March 3, 2012 at 11 am Gladys Levi was pronounced dead. My heart was broken but I could hear her voice, "It's time for you to do what you do!"

The boys traveled home and the preparations were made. The funeral services were beautiful just like my mom would have wanted. It took two weeks to sink in she was gone. One day I couldn't get out of bed and cried all day long. Greg never complained he just held me. The next week I heard my Mom's still small voice again, "Get up, get back to the journey. Tyler and Dev are young men now and I am with the Lord."

That very day I received an email requesting my services to be the key note speaker for the Women of Color Conference in Boston. After speaking with the publisher she offered a cover story and two other conferences in Dallas and Chicago. The Las Vegas Stars were preparing for their National Tour and a few Celebrity Basketball Games. The

National High School Basketball Association CEO called and asked me to set up basketball camps for High School students. Lastly, the development of the New American and International Basketball League was on the way. It was time to get back to the Boardroom and the Locker Room.

ABOUT THE AUTHOR

Alexis Levi is the First African American woman to own and act as CEO and General Manager of a Men's Professional Basketball team. She was the General Manager, CEO and Owner of the Las Vegas Stars Basketball team for the 2007 and 2008 seasons with the International Basketball League. She has written "Alexis Levi: Boardroom to the Locker room: The First African American Woman to own a Men's Professional Basketball Team.

She wrote the book in an effort to inspire all people to strive for their God given destiny and purpose despite the odds, cost or challenges. She experienced with unwavering faith first hand the personal cost of stepping into her dreams despite insurmountable obsticles, and horrific battles. In the end only to be amazingly surprised by victory, open doors and unceasing opportunity. She lives in the San Francsico, Bay Area. She is an entrepreneur and forerunner in many respects. She is from the San Francisco, Bay Area and resides in the Bay Area and Las Vegas. She is also a mother of two boys Deavereaux and Tyler.

To Contact Author:
Alexis Levi
alexislevi@gmail.com
For the Las Vegas Stars
thelasvegasstars@yahoo.com
For 2013 Celebrity Basketball Schedule:
thelasvegasstars@yahoo.com
Internet address: alseg1.wix.com/alexislevi
For Sports for Life: alseg1.wix.com/sportsforlifeusa

For Speaking Engagements and requests, please email alexislevi@gmail.com

For proposed topics of discussion: alseg1.wix.com/alexislevi#!alexis-speaks

For the Updated 2013 tryout schedule: thelasvegasstars@yahoo.com

For Team Development, Sports Marketing, Player Development, marketing and branding development. Contact alexislevi@gmail.com

For Website Development and Production services: Alexis Levi Productions.

American International Professional Basketball Association Information. alexislevi@gmail.com

UPCOMING BOOKS
- NO LIMITS NO BOUNDARIES
- ATHLETE 101
- PRO ATHLETE 101
- WOMEN IN THE SPORTS BIZ
- KEEP IT MOVIN
COMING SOON
PRO BALLER MAGAZINE: National Sports Magazine
HOTT SPOTT MAGAZINE: TV, Magazine and Social Media/
Video platform. Covers Music, Entertainment, TV, Sports and
more...........